STOCKINGS &
SUSPENDERS

Riddle: Why is
this called
the giggle line?

Answer: Because once you're there you're laughing.

STOCKINGS & SUSPENDERS

❦ ❦ ❦

A Quick Flash

ROSEMARY HAWTHORNE

Author of

Knickers: An Intimate Appraisal

Bras: A Private View

Drawings by Lucy Pettifer and Claire Taylor

Souvenir Press

The right of Rosemary Hawthorne to be identified as author of this work has been asserted by her in accordance with the Copyright, Designs and Patents Act 1988.

First published in Great Britain 1993 by Souvenir Press Ltd, 43, Great Russell Street, London WC1B 3PA and simultaneously in Canada

ISBN 0 285 63143 8

Photoset and printed in Great Britain by
Redwood Books
Trowbridge, Wiltshire

The author wishes to thank the following for their help in preparing this book: Mary Silverthorne, Mary Want (for her drawings), Margaret Ling, Pam Howarth, Valerie Threlfall, Jean White, Mary Warren, Valerie Mansell and Cynthia Noble. Also the hosiers, Messrs. Aristoc, Charnos, Brettles, Morley, Wolford and Wolsey and, in particular, all the kind ladies — and gentlemen — who have provided personal reminiscences that reveal so much about stockings and suspenders in the past.

The hosiery and suspenders illustrated in the book are part of the author's collection of period clothes.

The extracts from *Miss Manners' ® Guide to Excruciatingly Good Behaviour* by Judith Martin, copyright © 1979, 1980, 1981, 1982 by United Feature Syndicate, Inc., are reproduced by permission of Hamish Hamilton Ltd.

Every effort has been made to trace the copyright owners of material used in this book. The author and publisher will be glad to hear of any unintentional omission so that due acknowledgement may be made in any subsequent reprint.

CONTENTS

For Mary:
dearest blewstocking

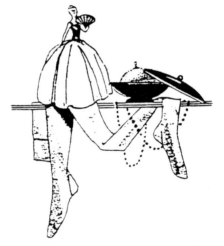

'Brevity is the soul of lingerie'
Dorothy Parker

PREFACE

Stockings and suspenders
Had a little lark
Played a game of 'Touch'
That was more fun in the dark.

When it was suggested that I should write a book about the history of stockings, garters and suspenders, my initial reaction was, there won't be much there (yawn) to get my teeth into. I couldn't have been more wrong. Lots of enthusiastic leg-work has led me to understand, enjoy and respect all three of these items in a way I wouldn't have thought possible.

If you believe that stockings all look like each other — and always have done — then think again. They are the historical chameleons of fashion, changing their appearance time and time again to fit in with what is 'going on' up top.

Garters deserve all the paeons of praise going, and in former centuries they got them. Poets waxed lyrical about garters — which is more than they ever did about suspenders.

Suspenders and stocking-tops! They still send a thrill of anticipation around the music-halls and school changing-rooms. I think of suspenders as a gallant troupe of hard-working show girls who have given us lots of pleasure in their time, who never let us down ... well, hardly ever ... and always get their man!

Here, then, is a skirt-lifting look at history. Find out why Elizabeth the First didn't want to get her feet wet in a puddle, and why Fanny Hill practised her garter business to perfection — and why, above all, boys have always loved to ping the 'suspies'.

It's a history lesson you'll not forget, I'm sure.

R.H.

Pair of stockings which belonged to Queen Victoria

A pair of pale, pearl pink silk stockings that belonged to Queen Victoria: almost as sheer as modern nylon, they date from about 1840 and may have been part of her wedding trousseau.

The letter 'P' in the welt is for Paris, although English hosiers, including Morley, George Brettle, and Allen & Solly (now Aristoc), also supplied the Queen. The crown and initials (and 'set' number — Victoria would have ordered these by the dozen) are made by transferring stitches by hand during the looming. The simple arrowhead clocks are beautifully hand embroidered and the back seams are neatly oversewn.

These exquisite stockings are the pride and joy of my collection.

ONE

STARTING FROM SCRATCH

His hose took sixteen hundred and fifty-seven yards and a third of light wool material, and were slashed in the form of ribbed pillars, indented and notched behind so as not to overheat his kidneys...

From *The Histories of Gargantua and Pantagruel.* Rabelais

Would it surprise you to learn that stockings are over 3,000 years old? Their history is closely linked to that of knitting — from the Saxon *cnyttan*, to make fabric with thread by hand — and this simple craft was being practised in the Middle East well before the reign of Cleopatra. Nomadic tribes of Arabia knitted sandal socks on simple 'pegged' knitting frames, similar to the cotton-reel bobbins that children still enjoy today as 'French knitting'. The women spun the yarn and the men did the knitting.

It is fascinating to think of the glamorous, sexy, Cleopatra having to wear socks to keep the sand out of her toes.

A gradual change-over from a pegged frame to bone or wooden needles took place in Arabia during the lifetime of Christ and it was from then on that the craft spread, via Christian missionaries who carried their portable hobby with them from country to country.

The sea traders acquired examples of knitting, which explains how the skills sailed rapidly to Spain where eventually some of the most beautiful and sophisticated forms of knitting originated. By the eleventh century AD Spain had become the centre of hand-knitted silk hose. This fashionable influence then sped onward to France and other countries in Europe — with the notable exception of the British Isles. During this period knitting remained intimately associated with the clergy and the choicest work was intended to adorn the priests.

The Church continued to benefit throughout the Middle Ages as professional knitting in Europe developed to an increasingly high standard. Two or more needles were used to make fine stockings and ecclesiastical gloves worked in silk with coloured motifs, while at the other end of the spectrum peasants knitted themselves rough woollen caps and other simple garments from a coarse yarn called 'sprang'.

Hose, although this word was not used in the limited sense of stockings until the seventeenth century, came in two sizes in the early years — long, to the thigh, if you were rich, and short, barely to the knee, if you were poor. There is a thirteenth-century French painting of Kings Caspar and Melchior, two of the Magi, wearing thigh-length stockings (Melchior's particularly nice in black with gold motifs) with what looks like a couple of suspenders showing. And what

do you know ...? They are! Under their tunics there was a leather belt with tabs that attached to the stockings-tops. Trust the French to think of suspenders first. Then, like so many sensible, civilised arrangements, the whole idea got lost for about 600 years.

Both long and short hose were very brightly coloured, with banded stripes being most popular. We get frequent glimpses of these unisex stockings in Geoffrey Chaucer's *Canterbury Tales*, including the lines on the splendid Wife of Bath:

> Hir hosen weren of fyn scarlet reed,
> Ful streite y-teyd.

Not all stockings were of knitted yarn. In Britain as elsewhere, most were made from material, cut on the cross. These 'cut hose' (or cut-ups) were probably of the same pattern as worn by an order of French nuns from the fifteenth century until 1970. The nuns' habits, based on medieval peasant dress (humble and hard-wearing) included stockings or 'chausses' (tight coverings for legs and feet) of bias-cut cloth or homespun made in two distinct types, for winter and summer: one of twilled wool, the other stout linen. Both were hand-stitched with generous seam allowances.

When completed these tailored stockings were so thick and stiff that they stood, unaided, like a pair of boots. Were they comfortable? We don't know ... but in 1490 there was a little rhyme that went:

> She hobbles as a gose
> In her blanket hose.

Chausses sometimes had tie-strings to hold them in place, but short hose could also be simply gartered below the knee. Male long-hose of this period had a more complicated arrangement: the upper border, or welt, was pierced with eyelet holes through which strings were threaded and then passed through corresponding holes in the tunic or doublet. In effect, these were another early form of suspenders (ah, but not as nifty as those of the Three Wise Men), called 'points'. The whole procedure was known as 'trussing the points'.

Young men at this time displayed, to the full, their manly limbs and other male attributes — so it is not surprising that, ere long, the hose, having become extremely long, were joined at the crotch, continuing over the hips to form 'upperstocks' or 'tights' that at first barely covered the wearer's seat; the ballet is forever indebted to this fashion of riveting virility as this little poem illustrates:

> When Nureyev and Margot were dancing,
> Just swanning around on the floor,
> He caught his tights on a backdrop
> And was seen to be Rudi some more.

Increasingly these tights began to fasten to the ever-shortening doublet with the same trussing method as before, although now the points were often tipped with ornamental metal tabs called 'aiglets'. Brightly dyed hose, often parti-coloured, were fashionable — thus one leg could be dark, the other light, or one leg zig-zagged while its partner had vertical stripes.

Dress design exercised every ingenuity in the matter of contrast and expense — as a character declares in a contemporary play: 'Indeed, there's reason there should be some difference in my legs, for one cost me twenty pounds more than the other.'

By the end of the fifteenth century the portion of tights covering the male posterior was called the 'trawses' or 'breach' and this could be made of a different material and decoration from the legs, thus giving the illusion of a separate garment . . . but that, ladies and gentlemen, is another story.

TWO

FIT FOR A QUEEN

'Where be my stockens? ... I will have no more woorsted
hosen, showe me my Carnation silk stockins: where laid you
last night my garters?'
    Lady Ri-Mellaine in *The French Garden*. Peter Erondell

The woollen trade, without doubt, was a most profit-
able and formative influence in British history. Once
the knitting craft was established in England even the
humblest of families could earn 'a bit extra' in their
own homes. By the late fifteenth century knitted
garments were part of everyday fashion, and with the
founding of the knitting Guild became not just a craft,
but art. As with embroidery, tapestry and lace-
making, men dominated the Guild — women were
only admitted as widows to keep alive the skills of
their departed husbands.

An apprentice knitter had to achieve a formidable
technique with the 'pins' before he was made a
Member. For three years a boy learned the rudiments
of the craft after which he was sent abroad to study, in
depth, the various forms of sophisticated knittery developed in other countries. At the end of his time he
must produce, for examination, a shirt, a felted cap, a
pair of stockings with fancy clocks, and a carpet. A far
cry from the knit one, purl one school of clickers!

Italy was one of the places a high-flying knitting
student would certainly have visited. In 1562 Eleanor
of Toledo, an Italian aristocrat, was buried in Florence
wearing not only superb, costly clothes but a magnificent pair of hand-knitted red silk stockings with

woven garters. A woman of this importance would have known the luxury of such stockings from child-hood — whereas poor Queen Elizabeth I, unlike her contemporary French, Italian and Spanish counter-parts, had to make do with the old cut-ups which fitted badly and lacked the nice clinging quality of hand-knitted silk.

Master Henry Herne was the Queen's hosier, supplying bias-cut hose in cloth, linen and, occasionally, silk.

The Queen loved dancing her galliards 'high', in the Italian manner, wearing fashionable dresses with wide skirts that showed the feet and trim ankles, so it is no wonder that, as a young woman, she craved a more appealing leg-covering than Master Herne's 'stitched Sarcenett' which, although a thin silk material, would have wrinkled in an unattractive way.

She must have been persistent in her quest for knitted silk, because in 1562 — by coincidence the year Eleanor turned up her toes — it is recorded that on New Year's Day, when traditionally presents, including clothes, could be offered to the monarch, Robert Robotham, Yeoman of the Wardrobe of Robes, presented her with 'two paire of black sylke hose knytt', and in the following year, lo and behold, he repeated the gesture.

Now these were likely to be imported goodies (all the courtiers were inclined to be secretive and played 'personal service to Elizabeth' cards close to their chests), since it is Mrs Alice Montagu, 'the Queen Majestie's silke woman', who is credited with having made and given the first pair of English hand-knitted silk stockings to Elizabeth. This was in 1564 when the Queen was 31 years old — just the age when a woman likes to feel at her elegant best. Elizabeth was so enchanted with this gift that the donor, reputedly using as a pattern a pair of Spanish silk hose that had been given to Elizabeth's late half-brother, Edward, by a courtier, Sir Thomas Gresham, promised her mistress that she would 'presently set more in hand'. The Queen's reply is recorded: 'Do so, for I like silke stockings so well because they are pleasant, fine and delicate and henceforth I will wear no more cloath stockings.'

Mrs Montagu was as good as her word and in the following year produced more luxury stockings, plus 'a paire of Taphata garters being edged at thendes with depe golde fringe'.

Lucky Bess!

However, it is pretty obvious that Mrs M. wasn't a very fast knitter as, going back on her word, Elizabeth

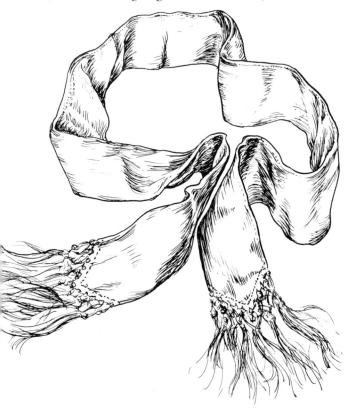

did order more pairs of cut-ups from Henry Herne (possibly to wear in colder weather or as 'protectors' for her silk). Six pairs of cloth hose were delivered in 1568, and in 1571 he made a further 'eleven paire of cloth Hose doble welted with vellat and lyned with sarceonett stitched with silke'. The velvet welts were doubled over the stocking-tops for strength.

Small wonder, remembering how thick these stockings must have been, that Elizabeth took up the offer of Sir Walter Raleigh's cloak to avoid stepping into *that* puddle; a pair of Henry Herne's would have been an age drying out...

Alice Montagu also made a pair of 'Norwich worstede yarne knytt hose' — woolly ones — for Elizabeth in 1577, and after that her mistress seems finally to have left off wearing the old-fashioned cut and stitched stockings. She liked to be up to date, and now wore a selection of coloured silk hand-knits — which had to be clean and well-mended. 'Looke well if the stockings have any stitches broken in them' was her constant reminder, and the hosiers, not the laundresses, had the job of washing these precious things since it was thought to be beyond the skills of those only used to handling tough linen sheets.

The Queen's sartorial vanity was huge — unlike her poor cousin, Mary, Queen of Scots, who went to the scaffold on a cold day in February 1587 wearing a pair of old-fashioned worsted stockings which Elizabeth would not have been seen dead in. It was the royal lust for more and finer silk hose, coupled with the plea 'that this new fashion of mine bring up a new trade in which many of my people may be employed', that eventually led to the establishment of the hosiery trade in England.

THREE

THE KNITTING VICAR

Kneeling ne'er spoiled silk stockings; quit thy state;
All equal are within the Church's gate.

George Herbert

In 1560, about the time we suspect Elizabeth of first
yearning for superior silk hand-knits, William Lee was
born in Nottingham. In due course, he was ordained
and became the Reverend William Lee, MA, Curate
of Calverton, Nottinghamshire.

Like so many worthy clerics, besides the weekly
Cure of Souls and perpetual spiritual leadership of his
flock, he was an ardent pursuer of a more practical,
hands-on pastime to add balance — and money — to
his life. William Lee was an inventor and, with the
help of his brother James, an engineer, he designed a
frame knitting machine that could manufacture
stockings.

This was the first mechanical stocking-loom.

Lee is entitled to rank among the few original
inventors the world has ever seen — they are rare
beings. No mechanical device for knitting had previously been constructed, or even thought of; he had to
form the idea and work out its practical shape without
any preconceived notion of what his loom should
look like. It is said that he devised it after watching his
fiancée absorbed in knitting a neat heel onto a worsted
stocking. With one needle holding the loops, the
lady's deft fingers quickly made a new series of stitches
on the other. From these observations he designed a
frame that made robust, knitted woollen stockings

which only needed closing by hand down the back seam. In 1589, the cleric took his prototype and demonstrated it before the Queen, but Elizabeth wasn't impressed — or if she was she kept quiet about it. She refused to make Lee a grant of money, secure a monopoly for him or a patent to work under her patronage, complaining that the loom's rustic product did not compare with the fine, silk hand-knits she'd grown used to wearing.

'I have too much love of my poor people, who obtain their bread by the employment of knitting, to give money toward an invention which will tend to their ruin, by depriving them of employment and thus make them beggars,' said she ... and, furthermore, 'Had Mr Lee made a machine that loomed silk stockings, I should, I think, have been somewhat justified in granting him a patent for that monopoly, which would have affected only a small number of my subjects, but to enjoy the exclusive privilege of making stockings for the whole of my subjects, is too important to grant to any individual.'

In other words, Elizabeth, although short-sighted as a businesswoman, quite rightly concluded that, as a monarch, she had better play safe: the invention would be the death of the hand-knit industry as it stood, and she would be held responsible.

Lee was bitterly disappointed at his monarch's dismissive attitude, but he returned to Calverton and continued to improve his machine in the vain hope that Elizabeth might see fit to help him at a future date.

Maybe they were all blind to the potential this invention offered, or perhaps the Queen just had too many pairs of stockings. Whatever the reason, this work remained unrecognised in England. Later, Lee designed a loom that could cope with silk, and eventually he emigrated with his frames to Rouen in France, where once again he sought royal patronage.

Henri IV of France was most impressed by the invention and promised support, but unfortunately was assassinated before his seal could be set on the contract. France was then too occupied with her own internal problems to give an immigrant inventor much comfort (Lee may even have been thrown into prison), so although he produced several viable frames before he died, in about 1611, he remained a rejected, impoverished man and was buried in an unmarked grave near Paris.

After his death his brother James, who had gone with him to France, returned to England and set up the craft of framework knitting. Slowly, almost imperceptibly, the stocking-making skills took root in London's East-end (the centre of the silk mercers' trade and where all the posh clothes were made), and then moved up into the Home Counties and on into the East Midlands ... firstly to Leicester, then Derby and, lastly, Notthingham, the birthplace of the originator.

Meanwhile the looms — and know-how — that Lee had left in France went on to provide the basis for the French stocking industry, a manufactured product that was to dominate the world of hosiery by the end of the nineteenth century. History is full of irony!

In 1663, almost a hundred years after the invention of the stocking-loom, a charter was granted by Charles II to form a Guild of Framework Knitters — so the Reverend William Lee's creation was at last honoured.

During the next two centuries the declining hand–knit trade was forced to move farther and farther north into the more primitive and rural areas. It managed to survive as a cottage industry in the Yorkshire Dales, on sparsely populated islands and in other untravelled parts of the British Isles, and was further helped during the lean years of the nineteenth century, when full mechanisation came to areas of textile looming, by a succession of wars when comforts for the troops were needed.

'Socks, socks, socks for the soldier boys,' sang the children as the needles flew back and forth along the rows of stitches ... well, as always, it's a mean wind that blows no one any good...

FOUR

CROSS-GARTERING, SLOPS, CLOCKS AND BOOT-HOSE

He will come to her in yellow stockings, and 'tis a colour she abhors; and cross-gartered, a fashion she detests.
Twelfth Night. William Shakespeare

Since in former times it was men — not women — who persistently revealed their hose-clad legs, it is their sartorial peculiarities we need to examine for further enlightenment on the evolution of stockings.

The prevailing fashionable 'image' for upper-crust men of the sixteenth and early seventeenth centuries was very macho: an important, puffed-up torso, slim waist and strong hips tapering down to sleek legs with pronounced calves and neat ankles. Balancing the width of the body, an 'uncommon pretty' pair of slender masculine legs was essential, and many notions were introduced to accentuate such a feature, of which cross-gartering was but one.

The practice of cross-gartering over the hose went back hundreds of years to a time when 'leg bandages' of linen or wool had been wound over stockings from the ankles to just below the knee. Worn like puttees, with the ends tucked in or tied, these often replaced hose entirely. Both peasantry and gentry bandaged — the peasants for protection, the gentry for decoration. Criss-crossing was an arrangement confined to royal or ecclesiastical circles, and the whole look was re-

vived with gusto by the young nobles in the second half of the sixteenth century.

Hoping to draw attention to a well-formed leg cased in (fairly) wrinkle-free netherstocks, cross-gartering was executed thus: the garter, now made of wide silk ribbon, was placed below the front of the knee, the ends passed back and given a cross-twist behind the knee to be tied in a large bow at the side or,

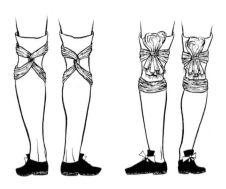

occasionally, the front. The prime example of this style is the poor, duped Malvolio in Shakespeare's *Twelfth Night* — but these accessories were not, please note, spiralled down the leg like garden trellis, as is done in so many productions of this play!

Elizabethan silk stockings were madly expensive. A tailor's bill of 1600 enters, 'Pd. for a paire of silke stockings for him, 25s,' which was big bucks at the time.

As I have mentioned, the term 'hose' meaning stockings is ambiguous until 1660, when it was finally accepted to mean, for men, only socks or stockings; during Elizabeth's reign it usually referred to breeches as well. For women, the word 'stockings' was fixed, and meant just that, by about 1550.

There was another curious Elizabethan fashion, wholly male, called trunk-hose (also known as slops or galligaskins, just to confuse you!) These were part of a two-piece suit, consisting of a bombasted (padded) doublet designed to create a huge 'peascod belly', like that of Mr Punch, worn with a pair of breeches, equally baggy and bombasted (even, so I read, slashed and pricked), which stopped at the knees where they were attached to a pair of fine stockings, thus making a single garment — trunk-hose.

The bombast effect was achieved by stuffing with rags, wool, tow, hair and even bran, and there is a delightful story of a young man who, engaged in sprightly, animated conversation with a group of ladies, caught his trunk-hose on a nail and let out a stream of bran. The hose collapsed to the consternation of the wearer and the vast amusement and delight of the ladies!

The rich aristocrats remained faithful to this cumbersome fashion until the arrival of Charles I — a man of taste and handsome with it — whereupon the big bellies and trunk-hose perceptibly shrank. However, fops continued to have regard for the state of their legs and, for several decades more, wore false calves 'when required'.

The odd terms 'clocks', 'clocking' and 'quirks' refer to the decoration or embroidery on either side of the stockings, which particularly enhances the ankle or lower leg. The words are recorded as early as 1530 (and even today a hosiery manufacturer would know what you were talking about), but the origin is obscure. The word 'clock' is thought to describe the 'hands of a clock' or arrowhead design which is commonplace. It was a decorative technique first used on tailored stockings to disguise the ugly 'fitted' seams at the ankle. 'Gore' clocks were separate, inserted wedge shapes, again used to assist the fit, and could be six or seven inches high. Both men and women loved the over-the-top embellishment of their stockings in the sixteenth and seventeenth centuries and there are some wonderful paintings showing them off. I love the portrait in the Victoria and Albert Museum of Richard Sackville, Earl of Dorset, painted in 1616, showing his lordship in a snazzy pair of bright blue silk hose, with splendid clocks of gold thread on the inner and outer turn, ankle to mid-calf.

Boot-hose were another way to command leg-attention if you were a fella. These were over-stockings that protected the finer, more expensive

'underhose' from contact with the rough inner surface of the boots. They had superb decorated tops, which perched above or turned over the top of the said boots and were exquisitely bordered with embroidery. Since they were a luxury item, they were detachable and could be used on different pairs of over-stockings as needed.

So far in our story it is men who have controlled the quaint vagaries manifest in a pair of stockings, although during the seventeenth century women's stockings were similar in every way — except they were not seen (much) publicly after about 1625, when skirts descended to floor-sweeping length and remained thus for the next 50 years. Everything gets a lot jollier, lighter and prettier when Charles II comes

home from exile in a pair of hilarious petticoat breeches.

In his time Charles was intimate with many feminine stockings and garters. For a start there were those of his wife, Catherine of Braganza, possibly a bit stiff and starchy, but I daresay those worn by his mistresses, Lady Castlemaine, Lady Portsmouth, Lucy Walker and, especially, Nell Gwyn ... were a lot easier to handle ...

> Nelly was a Welsh girl
> Nelly met a King;
> Nelly knew her oranges
> And saved the best for him

Throughout the eighteenth century hose — for both sexes — continued to become more attractive, sophisticated and comfortable. They could be hand-knitted or machine-loomed, and although many older men tended to keep to the tailored variety of their youth, the young gallants now wore ribbed, diced and 'chequered' hose. Materials used in stocking-making were cotton, wool yarn, jersey, worsted or silk, and the colours red, scarlet, blue, brown, ash and grey were popular, but a correctly dressed professional or upper-class man would have worn black for all occasions other than weddings or full evening dress, when white was *de rigueur*. Women's stockings reached to just above the knee and were knitted, in fine or coarse 'thread', worsted, cotton, wool, silk and — very special — cobweb silk. A novel idea was introduced during 1755 when an advertisement in the *Salisbury Journal* advises that 'Ladies ... may have their own name wrought in the stocking whilst weaving'.

One girl who probably wouldn't have cared a toss about her name was the prostitute in a marvellous painting by William Hogarth, 'The Rake at the Rose Tavern'. She is shown sensuously undressing — in public — and her stockings are blue with scarlet zigzags and a coronet above the gore clocks. A present from a noble client? Or pinched? Or bought as cast-offs at Rag Fair? We don't know — all we realise is that these smart stockings do a big PR job and give her legs the attention she demands. The girl's garters are also scarlet . . . in keeping with her profession.

At the other end of the social scale we have nice Jane Austen, an arbiter of taste for the gently-born, who had a distinct weakness for stockings and often mentions them in her novels and in letters to her sister, Cassandra:

> You say nothing of the silk stockings. I flatter myself, therefore, that Charles [Fowle — a close friend of the family] has not purchased any, as I cannot very well afford to pay for them; all my money is spent buying white gloves and pink persian. [Persian was thin silk used for lining.]

Interesting to see that in 1796 a worldly young man could be encouraged to buy a girl a pair of stockings without being thought at all impudent.

FIVE

BLUE-STOCKINGS
AND FOPS

> But oh, Sir, at our grand dinner, a young minx of quality sat
> near me and a gentleman told me she was very clever, and
> wore blue stockings: I did not know what that had to do with
> her cleverness...
>
> Spoof letter to the Editor, *The World of Fashion*, 1824.

This is the moment when we must mention blue-stockings, a term that is nowadays used somewhat derisively to refer to women who have literary, scholarly leanings that make them appear unfeminine. Stuff and nonsense!

Naturally, this misconception at first arose because it had been a man who coined the name – but to be fair, originally he had been levelling his sarcasm at both sexes.

In about 1400 a society was formed in Venice of intellectual ladies and gentlemen who distinguished themselves by wearing blue-coloured stockings. By 1590 this salon was finished in Italy but going strong in Paris, where the Bas-bleu Club was all the rage among the lady *savantes*. From France it crossed the Channel to England in the eighteenth century, where they already had a sneaking regard for 'blew-stockingism' — aligned to certain left wing political viewpoints and sober authorship. In London the official Bluestockings started in 1750 with assemblies that included women and met at Montague House, where they substituted smart literary conversation for game-playing, cards, gambling and general horse-play.

The principal attendant at these meetings was Mr Benjamin Stillingfleet, who habitually wore the more down-market blue worsted stockings instead of the usual gentlemanly black silk. In reference to this scandalous sartorial aberration the whole *côterie* were spitefully dubbed by Admiral Boscawen (who was decidedly black silk only) the 'Bluestocking Society' and the name stuck ... to the women!

There was a lot of satire in the eighteenth century, some of it very cruel — writers and playwrights had no qualms about subjecting the foibles of High Society to public scrutiny. Often it was conceived solely as a bit of allowable, spot-on-target fun for the punters. Clothes and 'how they wear 'em' were fair game ... and stockings were not immune:

Lord Foppington: The calves of these stockings are thickened a little too much; they make my legs look like a porter's . . .

Mr Mendlegs: My lord, me thinks they look mighty well.

Lord Foppington: Ay, but you are not so good a judge of these things as I am. I have studied them all my life. Pray therefore let the next be the thickness of a crown-piece less.

Mr Mendlegs: Indeed, my lord, they are the same kind I had the honour to furnish your lordship with in town.

Lord Foppington: Very possibly, Mr Mendlegs; but remember that was in the beginning of winter; and you should always remember, Mr Hosier, that if you make a nobleman's spring legs as robust as his autumn calves, you commit a monstrous impropriety, and make no allowance for the fatigues of winter.

That was R. B. Sheridan in his version of Vanbrugh's *The Relapse*, which he renamed *A Trip to Scarborough*.

In the last quarter of the century there was a sudden great passion for stripes, both vertical and horizontal. This was the preferred hose of the 'Marconis', a club formed of aesthetic young men who, having done the grand tour of Italy, took on a distinctive, albeit foppish mode of dress that included long, gleaming curls and quizzing glasses. They were the sartorial first cousins of the 'Jessamies', another raffish group (originators of the contemptuous saying of my grandparents' generation, 'He looks like a Jessy') who wore not only the curls, quiz and lots of stripes, but also gloves delicately scented with jasmine. Gorgeous, huh?

SIX

THE CIRCLET OF HONOUR

'Fast and Loose', an Elizabethan cheating game. Also known as 'Prick the Garter'.

No matter if hose was widely worn, more available, better loomed and, if necessary, beautifully decorated — the plain fact is that stockings, as worn by women, during the first eighteen centuries cut no erotic ice whatsoever.

In the eighteenth century the bosom held sway; this was the centrepiece of sex appeal, and a fair and shapely bosom, particularly if it heaved, could turn a young — or old — man's fancy!

A mature Dr Samuel Johnson in 1750 was to observe to his friend David Garrick, the actor: 'I'll come no more behind your scenes, David, for the white silk stockings and white bosoms of your actresses excite my amorous propensities.'

So perhaps the intellectuals were already getting there.

But garters ... ah, now, they were a different story entirely.

Garters were loaded with sexual innuendo, with subliminal invitation and the promise of physical 'advancement'. There are endless references to support their erotic appeal — poetry, prose, letters, diaries, illustrations, paintings and plays — all highlighting the aura of enticement that surrounded the garter, and the act of gartering and ungartering by a woman.

The most famous garter in the land, worn by the

twenty-four Knights of the Garter, the highest chivalric honour bestowed in England, came into being because of a symbolic gesture from a man to a woman.

This garter of blue velvet, worn below the left knee, is reputed to commemorate an incident in 1348, at a ball in Calais celebrating the defeat of the town. King Edward III, dancing with the Countess of Salisbury with whom he was in love, saw one of her garters fall to the ground. To save her further embarrassment and dishonour, he picked it up and, ignoring the nudge, nudge, wink, wink jokes from his watching friends, tied it around his own left knee and uttered the famous words, '*Honi soit qui mal y pense*' (Shame on him who thinks evil of it).

It takes a charmer to say the right thing at the right time.

In order to solve the delicious problem of what lay above the garter-line a chap had a few options open to him: he could take a quick peep as she tied her garter, he could romp wildly with her until she fell down (there are lots of 'bottoms up' incidents in seventeenth- and eighteenth-century books and paintings)

or, as a much used ploy he could push his beloved on a swing.

Thus, swinging became a very popular pastime for lovers: many a Celia, Sylvia, Julia, Phyllis and the teasing rest played 'Now you see it, now you don't' from the safety of a garden swing. There were also other, less subtle ways:

Make your petticoat short that a hoop eight
  yards wide
May decently show how your garters are tied.

But you can take it from me that a clever woman had simpler, more effective ways of showing what she was made of.

Fanny Hill embodies the very essence of a go-getting garterer. The rumbustious heroine and 'Woman of Pleasure' of John Cleland's novel is an excellent interpreter of what was thought to be insatiably sexy in the eighteenth century (Madonna, eat your heart out). Fanny, bless her, is forever dressing and undressing, tumbling in and out of caps, gowns, shifts, stays and petticoats in the earnest pursuit of pleasing her men.

Never once, throughout her steamy, hands-on memoirs, does she even bother to mention stockings — whereas a 'neat leg' that had 'slipt its garter', which she made no scruple of tying before him, is an allusion strong enough to elicit a physical response from the male onlooker — and reader — alike.

Garters were the key to heaven's gate, the desired trophy for a lover, and at a time when knickers were entirely unknown (Fanny certainly didn't wear them), the area beyond the garter represented the whole field of conquest. The would-be lover had only to overcome the slight social obstacle of the circlet around the knee, which by the accepted protocol of the time was as insurmountable as a pair of directoire bloomers!

The semi-disclosure, in public, of a woman's garter therefore takes on tremendous meaning in the early centuries — at once come hither and provocative, yet also psychologically restrictive, a 'No Go' area. For the ardent suitor it was certainly tough reading the signals, but the expression 'casting her garter' was used into the early twentieth century to mean that a girl was hoping to hook a husband.

Garters were still made from lengths of ribbon and silk — Lyons in France and Coventry in England produced the best ribbons and braids that tied, or occasionally buckled, above or below the knee:

No matter if milk-white my stockings or no
Or whether I garter above or below.

Charmingly, garters often had pert designs or mottoes woven into them and these, naturally, were much hunted by bold explorers . . . so much so that women employed mock-severe entreaties to protect themselves: 'My heart is fixt, I cannot range,' says one garter, while another, from 1717, reads, 'I like my

love too much to change.' One from 1737 doesn't beat about the bush: 'No Search', it taunts.

By the end of the century the more daring and fashionable were putting their trust in garters that had small coiled springs of brass wire channelled into the padded lining. For the first time, this gave a certain elasticity.

The man who invented this technique was a surgeon dentist, Martin Van Butchell, who was living in Westminster in 1783 when he applied for a patent for 'spring bands or fastening for various purposes'. A former pupil of the famous Scottish surgeon, John Hunter, by 1769 he was already advertising artificial teeth with 'gold springs'. Somewhat eccentric (he rode a horse painted different colours and kept the body of his first wife embalmed in his house until his second wife, justifiably, complained), he was a great extoller of his own products and kept up a constant barrage of information about them, via public announcement.

In 1791, when Princess Frederica of Prussia married the Duke of York, second son of George the Third, Van Butchell advertised in a colourful print (an early poster), 'The Duchess Blush or York Flame', Van Butchell's Spring Garter — a bright red souvenir of the royal wedding!

Spring garters would have cost you 30/- per pair — a hefty price to pay for a fashion novelty in the eighteenth century — but, they did away with the risk of public disgrace when a loosely tied garter fell to become the prize of some unworthy rake.

SEVEN

LEGEND AND LORE

'Young ladies should take care of themselves. Young ladies are delicate plants. They should take care of their health and their complexion. My dear, did you change your stockings?'
Mr Woodhouse in *Emma*. Jane Austen

Various articles of clothing have traditionally attracted strong superstitions. Items such as gloves, shoes, stockings, shifts, garters, handkerchiefs, purses and buttons are all steeped in folklore, and of these shoes, stockings and garters are the trio that represent some firmly held beliefs relating to marriage.

In the seventeenth and eighteenth centuries shoes and stockings were symbols of good fortune. Shoes were thrown after the bridal pair as they departed on their new life together and even now are often tied to the back of the honeymoon car. Similarly, stockings were also 'tossed' at the happy pair.

The traditional practice of stocking-throwing is described by a Frenchman, Henri Misson, in 1698:

> The Bridegroom, who by the help of his Friends is undress'd in some other Room, come in his Night-Gown, as soon as possible to his Spouse who is surrounded by Mother, Aunt, Sister and Friends, and without further ceremony gets into Bed. The Bride-men take the Bride's stockings, and the Bride-maids the Bridegroom's. Both sit down at the Bed's Feet (backs to the bed) and fling the Stockings over their Heads, endeavouring to direct them so they may fall upon the married Couple. If the Man's stockings thrown by the Maid fall upon the Bridegroom's Head, it is a sign she will quickly be married herself; the same Prognostick holds good for Woman's stockings thrown by the Man.

This custom was still alive in Scotland in the nineteenth century. An eye-witness account of 1823 reports that the left stocking is flung — in folklore pairings the left so often appears to hold sway over the right.

By about 1850, although stocking-throwing was still part of the wedding day fun and games, the targets had changed and it was now the bride's turn to have a fling!

Garters were imbued with a different kind of luck. As you might expect, they were the romantic links with fertility. A bride's garters were terrifically important; they signified consummation, fulfilment, progeny, and always aroused fierce competition. In a play of 1700 a lady dressing for her wedding exclaims,

'I forgot my Bridall Garters ... O no, They're on! What striving there'll be about them ... and pinching one's leg.'

The untying of the nuptial garters was a deeply symbolic act. Henri Misson records that 'the Bride-men pull off the Bride's Garters, which she had before Unty'd that they might hang down and so prevent a curious Hand from coming too near her Knee. This done, the Garters being fasten'd to the Hats of the Gallants, the Bride-maids carry the Bride into the Bride Chamber, where they undress her and Lay her on the Bed.'

Can you imagine a wedding guest nowadays walking about wearing the bride's garters in his hat? Bridal garters were small, elegant sashes made of silk ribbon in pretty colours. Blue was popular, the colour of constancy, but red and white were also common. Green was considered unlucky and there is a story told in 1908 about a village near Balmoral, where, when a younger sister married before an elder, the latter was made to wear green garters at the wedding and became the quarry in a post-nuptial romp; any young man who had 'the taking of them off' was destined to be her future husband. No wonder, 'nay worn nor seen the colour o' green' ... it was obviously to be avoided!

Another romantic garter custom continuing well into the nineteenth century was for the youths to race from the church to the bride's house after the wedding ceremony and the first one to arrive could claim the right to remove the bride's left garter, which he would afterwards tie around his own true love's knee as a charm against unfaithfulness. Even now at weddings the photographer occasionally asks the bride to hitch

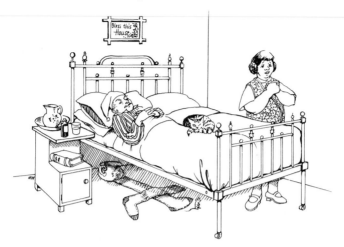

up her skirt and show off her garter (usually blue), and she may even remove it and throw it into the assembled company for someone to catch.

Eelskin garters cured the cramp and rheumatism — but you first had to catch your 'spring eels'! Stockings, too, had their magic powers. Hung crossed at the foot of the bed, with pins stuck in them, they kept away nightmares and bogey men. This 'cross' idea recurs throughout folklore, for shoes and gloves as well. A bride would only fall for a baby if the bridesmaids had been careful to place her stockings in a cross on her bed on her wedding night.

As a physic that cured, stockings sometimes had no equal. In the late 1930s a doctor was called to a cottage in Shropshire to attend a man who was very ill. He asked the man's wife what she had already done. 'Oh, doctor, there be naught that I 'unna done. I've even crossed 'is stockin's under 'is bed!'

Stockings could cure a sore throat (a dirty stocking, foot against the throat, wrapped round and kept on all night), or they could bring you a boy-friend. Nineteenth-century maidens in Buckinghamshire reckoned that the trick was to pin their stockings to the wall and recite:

> I hang my stockings to the wall,
> Hoping my true love for to call;
> May he neither rest, sleep, nor happy be,
> Until he comes and speaks to me.

Allowing for their lamentable lack of poetic rhythm, I hope it works. But what, after all, is the most well-known custom of the lot, centred on stockings? Why, Christmas stockings, of course!

EIGHT

THE FIRST FAINT BLUSH

Mistresses with great smooth marbly limbs.
                                    Robert Browning

From 1620 the development of William Lee's stocking frame ensured that hosiery became the staple industry for thousands throughout the country — particularly in the North. During the eighteenth century, stocking manufacture was the responsibility of the hose-master or hosier and he usually became a very wealthy man. He oversaw a clutch of frame knitters, called 'stockingers', to whom he rented the frames and who worked in their own homes. The looming of silk stockings was at first situated in London's Spitalfields, while the areas around Leicester, Nottingham and Derby continued to produce sturdier varieties of thread, wool and worsted.

The problem with these yarns was to keep enough spun to maintain the stockingers in full production — at a rough estimate it took eight spinners to provide enough yarn for one loom. In 1764, however, this shortfall was eased by the invention of James Hargreaves' spinning jenny, which allowed several spindles to be operated by a solo worker at one winding wheel. This idea was further improved beyond all measure by Richard Arkwright when he revolutionised the entire industrial concept with his design for a machine that spun quicker than man-power by using a steam-driven roller.

In France the stocking manufacturing areas were

Paris (fine silk), Rouen, Troyes and Lille (which is how we come by the word 'lisle' — it is a corrupted pronunciation). After the stockings were made, being finished with hand-sewn seams at the back (frame-knitted hose was made 'flat'), the hosier would sell them direct into the cities and big towns via an agent or would distribute them at a more lowly level by means of a haberdasher or bagman — a trader who dealt in all kinds of 'smalls' such as caps, hats, cuffs, thread, frills, ribbons and, of course, underwear.

Before the close of the eighteenth century, machines had been improved to such a degree that it was possible to loom net, ribbed, fleecy and 'elastic' (stretchy) materials for hose.  Thus, for all practical purposes, stockings at the dawn of the nineteenth century were a most sophisticated product. So perfect had Lee's original design been that his frames were still being used in the manufacture of stockings in 1800, and even now, after a myriad modifications (and computerisations), the basic principles that govern looming remain William Lee's concept.

At the beginning of the nineteenth century stocking frames were still being worked by hand; although there had been attempts at devising a simple drive mechanism to rotate the frame, none were successful until 1857 when a mechanically controlled rotary frame was introduced which not only knitted faster but also narrowed the fabric to the correct 'leg' shape.

But history reminds us that the gradual take-over of machinery from skilled labour reaped grim rewards. Vicious attacks were inflicted by the Luddites — organised groups of people who took part in systematic machine-wrecking riots in England between 1811 and 1816. Supposedly led by a General Ludd (although he may have been a fictitious character), the movement began in Nottinghamshire and spread quickly into the neighbouring counties. It was primarily a revolt against the unemployment caused by the introduction of faster-working machines. The rioters were hanged or transported — adding to the bitterness that artisans felt towards industrialisation.

The early 1800s were therefore anguished times for framework knitters. Machines stood idle, the workers too fearful to use them, and even the handful who dared take the risk earned only a pittance, so strict were the regulations applying to framework knitting. The workers and their families were made destitute — and they had never had it easy. A stockinger worked long hours, in a cramped hovel with blackened, oil stained windows, the rancid smell of the grease (called lather) that was used to lubricate the yarn seeping into his pores. Day and night the worn-out frames shook the house with their constant rumble, and yet the stockinger toiled on, knowing that he had to pay the hose-master's frame rent, on penalty of imprison-

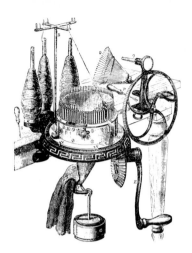

ment, and that charges were added for light, fuel and yarn with deductions for bad work.

It was the poet, Lord Byron, who headed a commission set up to investigate the plight of these poor, exploited workers. Gradually, the unremitting hardship improved as factories were built in the manufacturing towns and cities and jobs became available that employed large numbers of people full-time.

In essence, the shape and structure of women's stockings were to remain the same until the mid-nineteenth century. Stockings came to just above the knee and were made, as always, from cotton, fine wool or cashmere and silk if you were rich, and from more substantial fibres, such as lisle thread or worsted, if you were poor. Charming decorative clocks still accentuated the ankles of the well-to-do, and colours, from 1800, were 'quiet'; we read of a choice between olive, dove, grey or brown 'with yellow clocks' for day or walking dress, and black, white or pastel shades for afternoon or visiting clothes. White silk was still essential for evening dress, but pink was increasingly worn for less formal 'do's'.

So, at a time when fashionable dress for upper-class women favoured revealing shifts of high-waisted transparent muslin, recalling the classical folds of Ancient Greece, a comment of 1803 in *The Chester Chronicle* isn't far out: 'The only sign of modesty in the present dress of the Ladies is the pink dye in their stockings, which make their legs appear to Blush for the total absence of petticoats.'

Young men were now only wearing stockings as part of full evening uniform or court dress — tight pantaloon 'trowsers' had come into being — and strangely enough, as men's legs begin to retreat and have less prominent display, so women's stocking-clad legs start to catch the eye. Girl's legs under the flimsy frocks came in for close scrutiny, particularly on the dance floor — and certainly after the introduction of the waltz which was considered flagrantly unchaste and therefore very popular with the young!

The *Ipswich Journal* even reports that 'the German Waltz has become so general as to render the ladies' garters an object of consideration in regard to elegance and variety' — so one assumes that the Waltzing Matildas of the early 1800s exhibited quite a lot of leg as they circled the room.

Garters, now usually worn below the knee, were still able to make male hormones respond positively:

> Why blush, dear girl, pray tell me why?
> You need not, I can prove it;
> For tho' your garter met my eye
> My thoughts were far above it!

Blushing was the name of the game in the nineteenth century.

From 1820 until the 1840s it was 'correct' to wear coloured silk stockings with silk dresses and, likewise, 'openwork' cotton with 'sprigged' for light summer frocks. For balls or courtly occasions you were never wrong-footed in a pair of white silk with fine embroidered clocks. Women's shoes were entirely flat, like ballet slippers, so the wearer appeared to glide, swan-like, over the surface of the ground.

It was a twenty-year period that was romantically supercharged — the era of Victor Hugo, Sir Walter Scott, Edgar Allen Poe, and of Messrs. Byron, Keats, Shelley and Co, writers who thrilled and stirred the emotions of females until their hearts thundered with pleasurable excitement. The fashion changed to tight-waisted dresses with swelling, balloon-shaped sleeves and ever-widening skirts, the hems of which showed a neat ankle and a prettily shod foot. The effect was rather over-the-top and doll-like.

A magazine of 1835, two years before 18-year-old Victoria came to the throne, has confident views:

> If we wear thin stockings under prunella or kid shoes in winter we must expect that the natural state of the functions will be seriously disordered … Black stockings in winter, except for mourning, are in bad taste, unless the gown be black … they should, of course, always be silk … Garters which require tying ought to be loose … and if the calf of the leg is slender and the knee small — then two garters may be worn. Elastic garters are greatly preferred — some ladies attach two triangular pieces of elastic material to the straight edge of the corset and from each of these descend two tapes which, passing through a loop of tape attached to the stockings, render garters unnecessary.

Fine white cotton stockings with openwork decoration, 1830–65. The letter 'M', woven below the welt, denotes that the manufacturer was Morley, started in 1797 by John Morley with his brother Richard. The firm I. & R. Morley of Nottingham became internationally famous hosiers. They are now part of Courtauld's.

These stockings have loops to take buckled garters — and two large linen buttons (a later addition) to hold early elastic suspender 'loops'.

This last bit of advice, though it sounds fiddly, is of course an early shot at ... a suspender!

By the late 1840s, Victorian values stood solidly in place. The young Queen was mother to several children, and hearth and home were the main-spring of natural, middle-class contentment. Romance gave way to sentimentalism and women's clothes took on a meeker, heavier appearance, with emphasis on deep, full skirts that hid the wearer's feet entirely. Since female legs seem to disappear for the next few years, stockings become by-passed as objects unworthy of any attention, dismissed by the journals of the time; even a popular French novelist like Gustave Flaubert — the bodice-ripper of his day — who wrote the first 'hot' book about adultery (*Madame Bovary* was thought wildly indecent and Flaubert was tried for offending 'public morals' — no wonder the book became a romping success!) couldn't, in hundreds of pages of detailed description of what women wore, bring himself to mention stockings.

They had become, quite simply, unmentionables. Along with that other vital item of Victorian underwear, drawers, they withdrew from notice and the very thought of female lower limbs became taboo in mixed company.

NINE

WASHIN', MENDIN', DARNIN' ... AND THE KIDS

Thy young man is gone to sea
With silver buckles on his knee,
With his blue coat and yellow hose,
And that's the way the polka goes.

Traditional

Until the end of the nineteenth century, children's legs and how they were covered reflected, in miniature, the styles of grown-ups. White cotton stockings were worn by small girls until about 1855 when, as with their mothers, striped stockings in strong colours became increasingly fashionable. After 1870, black or brown in silk, lisle or wool were commonplace, worn even under the flimsiest white or pastel-coloured party frocks or summer dresses by upper- and middle-class girls, with black or bronze kid shoes, often purchased from Mr Daniel Neal's shop in the Edgware Road.

A reminder of what boys' hose was like in ye olden days remains as part of the uniform worn by pupils of the famous Blue Coat Schools. Of these,

Christ's Hospital is the earliest surviving charitable institution of its kind, founded in 1552. The benefactors who gave money to set up these schools — to soften the blow given to church-sponsored education during the Reformation — issued their selected, poor scholars with a distinctive uniform, based on the style of dress in vogue for children at that time. Christ's Hospital boys still sport the long blue buttoned coat, leather girdle, linen neckband (which has replaced the Tudor ruff) and a pair of yellow stockings (introduced in 1638), nicknamed 'mustard pots'. During ensuing centuries this archaic costume was copied by other charitably-minded worthies prepared to do good by setting up educational establishments for poor, often orphan, boys. Charles Dickens gives a pithy account of the 'Charitable Grinders' in his novel *Dombey and Son*.

Charity for girls had to wait until the late eighteenth and early nineteenth centuries — but here again, the 'uniform' conveyed a 'freezing' of the fashion at the time of founding. This idea, of course, was also true of the Foundling Schools and Workhouses. In *Jane Eyre* Charlotte Bronte describes the horrible Reverend Mr Brocklehurst on one of his rounds of inspection at Lowood school, giving close attention to domestic detail:

> I wish the woollen stockings were better looked to ... I went into the kitchen-garden and examined the clothes drying on the line; there was a quantity of black hose in a very bad state ... from the size of the holes in them I was sure they had not been well-mended.

Beast! But there you go: knitting, darning and mend-ing socks and stockings were some of the skills that personified the lower orders of womanhood up to the first half of the twentieth century. Every girl, from every walk of life, was taught to sew, but charity orphans sewed and knitted from the age of three to five, making things for the foundling babies. Charity boys sewed if they were to enter the tailoring trades or go to sea — but all boys could knit from the age of five.

The Workwoman's Guide, published in 1838, was the bible of practical sewing during Victoria's reign. It is entirely rational about the need to teach poor children to knit:

Knit stockings are considered so much better than woven ones for wear, that it is advisable for all servants, cottagers and labourers invariably to adopt them, as the former will last out three or more of the woven, which is more suitable for the higher classes.

The children of the poor should always be taught to knit, and each member of a family ought to have a stocking in hand to take up at idle moments.

Darning and mending are forgotten areas of needlework, but a perfectly darned hole, now such a rarity, was well known to generations of women and girls who occupied many hours carefully mending and darning the family clothes.

Such a darn is difficult to execute without a bit of know-how, patience and the right tools. You need a big darning needle (with a large 'eye'), darning wool or thread and a 'mushroom' — a piece of wood or plastic shaped like the vegetable — which you ram down the sock against the hole to create a firm base on which to cast your needle ... actually, generations of women in my family have used a hard, dried out orange, which is just as effective.

After which it's up to you!

By about 1840 the word 'socks' had become the accepted term describing hose for men and boys

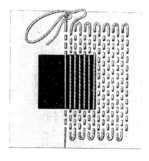
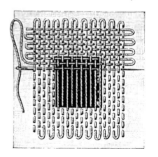

although for young girls it was not recognised until around 1880. From the second half of the century there were masses of wonderful patterns issued in magazines, perfect for every member of the family, whatever their age, status or occupation.

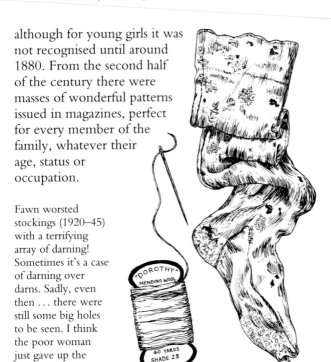

Fawn worsted stockings (1920–45) with a terrifying array of darning! Sometimes it's a case of darning over darns. Sadly, even then ... there were still some big holes to be seen. I think the poor woman just gave up the struggle ...

A winter bride's stockings, baby's first sock, father's day-wear socks, evening socks and his cycling and shooting stockings (these are 'stockings' because such hose is worn with breeches and the tops turn over the garters ... I bet you didn't know that). Excellent little books and pamphlets were published by the yarn-spinning firms, all containing up-to-date patterns and 'notions'.

For sheer enthusiasm my favourite is a chunky book, full of useful-things-for-girls-to-do, published

by the Religious Tract Society in 1900. Written by a middle-class matron, in a hearty, no-nonsense style, she occasionally smacks of Lady Bracknell: '. . . and, by the way, let me also remind you not to scamp anything you make for the poor. The "young lady's gift" will be well scrutinised by all the gossips in the neighbourhood. Though these good dames cannot do beautiful work themselves, they know how to appreciate it.' But it is in the art of re-heeling that our Matron shows true depth of understanding: ' "Ah!" some of my readers say, "it all reads well; but wait till you come to do it." Girls, such observations do not surprise me. I see failures of this kind happening daily. Sympathy does not excuse thoughtlessness . . . study the problem in hand.'

Washing the socks and stockings was another job that women were automatically selected to do. Woollen stockings were the worst to cope with: they needed gentle hand-washing in warm, sudsy water, with three rinses to clear the soap, and then had to be thoroughly wrung out through a towel, or mangled, and pegged, toe first, in the open air to dry. Silk hose were washed in soft water, rainwater being the best, with good soap, squeezed rather than rubbed and

then, if possible, a glass of gin was added in the final rinse before they were pulled into shape and dried flat. Afterwards it was advisable to rub them with a soft piece of flannel to bring up the lustre.

All coloured stockings were liable to fade, but black was the most difficult colour to wash and maintain. It was a fugitive dye and would readily streak. Not until the advent of a chemical dye (previously these had been vegetable), developed by Morley's with aniline salts in 1887, was this problem overcome and black hose no longer turned green or brown, or stained the feet the same hue.

There were some cunning ways of doing the family sock wash in a poor home. In 1900 a lady visited such a family at dinner time. 'A little lassie brought in a baked rice pudding, cooked in a small back kitchen. The mother noticed a peculiar odour, as the steam arose from the dish, and said, "Polly, the pudding has a queer smell." "Yes, mother," replied the child, "the stockings have boiled over on the oven shelf. But nothing went in the pudding for it was on the top, and the stocking pot was at the bottom." This was reassuring, but the soapy liquid having boiled over on the hot shelf had burned there, and raised sufficient steam and smoke to give the pudding an undoubted flavouring of essence of stewed stocking.'

Hardly ambrosia...

TEN

EXPOSE AND CONCEAL

Her feet beneath her petticoat,
Like little mice stole in and out.
Sir John Suckling

Between 1860 and 1870 we can detect an unmistakable frisson of excitement: women, perversely, had decided to reveal more than the toe-caps of their shoes.

This foot exposure — a re-tread of the last years of the 1600s when shortened skirts led to elaborately decorated stockings, high-heel shoes and poetic outbursts — created, yet again, the high-arched foot that was a perceived mark of pedigree. The oriental races

62

have always gone overboard about this, but as a Victorian *grande dame* was once heard to say, 'The Lower Orders all have flat feet!' — a sweeping statement that appeared, superficially, to have an irritating grain of truth.

A 'lady', real or aspiring, was at pains to present her feet in as dainty a way as possible, and a rising heel, supporting a pretty foot and ankle, dressed in eye-catching hose, was, suddenly, one of her most lady-like attributes. As the crinoline skirts grew to massive, unwieldy proportions over their hooped petticoats, the 'little mice' were seen scuttling about again. Plain white cotton or silk were usually worn with day-time 'house shoes', but coloured stockings were shod with the latest novelty, ankle boots. And what elegant footwear this was! Laced, buttoned or elastic-sided, the boots had names like 'Osborne', 'Balmoral' or 'The Imperatrice' (made of French satin with patent leather tips).

Equally splendid were the hose, which suddenly seemed to have caught an infectious disease. Spots appeared in rashes, all over the leg, monochrome or coloured on contrasting grounds, and there was an insatiable demand for circular stripes — to match the outer petticoat. After the death of the Queen's husband, Albert, in 1861, violet — in silk or cashmere — emerged as a fashion leader, doubtless out of respect for this sad event, but by 1865 strong colour was everywhere seen during daylight hours and there were reports of 'gas green gaiters and prunella boots' parading, unashamed, in Hyde Park. The Queen's passion for her Scottish home, Balmoral, stirred up veritable clans of Sassenachs — tartan supporters who had never so much as crossed the Border, let alone hill-walked in the Highlands. Soon enough, 'plaid' worsted stockings with 'ghillie' shoes were first-footing in Folkestone at the New Year, undoubtedly attracting lots of attention under the canopied skirts.

Certainly, much of the charm of croquet — that favourite pastime played in country house gardens throughout the British Isles and far-flung colonies — was that it focused male attention on a lady's feet.

Because of the need to get the mallet in a central position to strike that ball, it provided excellent opportunities for a coquettish display of 'lower limbs'. The 'inconvenience' of the enveloping skirt caused adjustments to be made: the top skirt was looped up in an artistic manner above the underlying petticoat, revealing — gasp! — the wearer's feet, ankles . . . and a little more beside.

A writer of 1867 comments: 'One of the chief reasons of the pleasure men take in this game is the sight of a neatly turned ankle and pretty boots'.

Fair enough!

The same technique held true for the dance floor: the waltz was now an established, respectable dance, but even so, swaying crinolines, momentarily tilted, exhibited much, and when boisterously swirled in a polka, much, much more. Fine, pastel-coloured silk stockings were still worn with evening dresses — their fragile beauty stored carefully, rolling-pinned flat, in

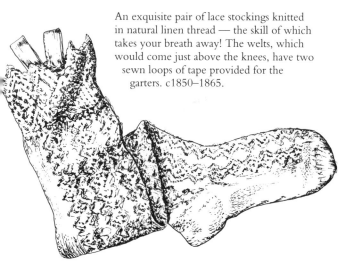

An exquisite pair of lace stockings knitted in natural linen thread — the skill of which takes your breath away! The welts, which would come just above the knees, have two sewn loops of tape provided for the garters. c1850–1865.

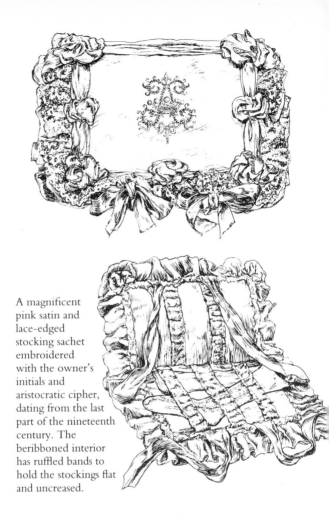

A magnificent pink satin and lace-edged stocking sachet embroidered with the owner's initials and aristocratic cipher, dating from the last part of the nineteenth century. The beribboned interior has ruffled bands to hold the stockings flat and uncreased.

fancy decorated and quilted sachets by their owners' maids. Such covers, normally part of a bride's trousseau, were often sumptuous — in satin and lace and sporting her 'new' initials. The idea of keeping good stockings 'safe' in special containers went out only after nylons became plentiful in the 1950s.

ELEVEN

ELASTIC — THE MAGIC WEB

Is there any dancing asked Mr Salteena.
Well not always said the Earl.
I am glad of that said Mr Salteena I am not as nimble as I
   was and my garters are a trifle tight.

The Young Visitors. Daisy Ashford

Not another move can I make without side-stepping, just a moment, to remind you what an incredible, uplifting difference the invention of elastic made to life . . . and to suspenders.

I'm rather smitten with elastic — it was vital to both knicker and bra history — but when you consider that our flexible friend took two hundred and fifty years to evolve from a gooey, black, resinous mess known as caoutchouc to the nice, user-friendly commodity that today holds up the world's knickers, well, perhaps, you can understand my hang-up.

Caoutchouc was discovered (in Brazil where the

nuts come from) in 1731 by a French scientist, Charles de la Condamine. He found natives making waterproof boots from this strange, milky substance which ran out from certain trees once the bark was cut, hardening on contact with air and turning black. However, de la Condamine's rubbery contribution to the civilised world is now possibly better commemorated by condoms than by gum boots!

Other plant families in Africa, Eastern Asia and India were also discovered to yield this wonderful milky stuff and were named 'elastica'.

Having collected your liquid rubber — or latex — the problem was to get it back home in a usable condition, the rubber being temperamental and liable to harden into useless blocks. The trick was to allow a certain amount of coagulation to take place and then ship it out quick so that it was manageable when it reached its destination for processing.

Many experiments in applying India-rubber solution to cloth were carried out, in the hopes of creating an effectively waterproofed material, but not until 1822 did one of these prosper. In the city of Glasgow, Charles Mackintosh tried softening caoutchouc in naptha and sandwiching it between two layers of cloth — so achieving the first impermeable material and founding an industry.

Initially 'mackintosh' was used for things like inflatable mattresses, cushions and life-belts, but it was far from trouble-free. The cloth was difficult to handle, the solution extremely volatile, and even under ordinary conditions it was very sticky, while heat rendered it oozy and smelly — and on cold days it just shrank and became hard as a plank of wood. It definitely wasn't a marketing man's dream product!

However, it so happened that in the early 1820s an Islington coachbuilder, Thomas Hancock, who was also a dab hand as an inventor, started to stitch little strips of 'mackintosh' into the wrists of coachmen's gloves (I know this seems miles off suspenders!) to give them a snug fit. Ten years later this neat idea was by-passed when an unknown German inventor introduced a thread of rubber into a woven web of fabric, to form a warp, and by keeping it in an extended state during weaving, and then releasing it, the fabric would be gathered up. Bingo! We have elastic!

Hancock, always a fly boy, quickly copied this idea in England, although he had his workers 'iron' the woven tape to bring back the spring . . . and he wasn't the only manufacturer working on British elastic: a Leicester hosiery and haberdashery firm owner, Caleb Bendells, also patented a method of elasticating knitted goods. So Leicester, already the home of stocking-making, opened its arms to elastic as a natural child into a happy family.

Elastic thread was expensive and time-consuming to make, but its novelty caught the imagination of inventors and designers, all eager to create a range of elasticated articles. It was still difficult to cope with: it lost all its stretchiness with constant strain, goods softened with heat and became brittle with cold, and it decomposed in a horrible way if exposed to sunlight or sweat.

Across the Atlantic the Americans were having just the same problems with the wretched stuff. By chance, in the year 1835, Charles Goodyear, a failed businessman and impecunious inventor, visited the Roxbury India Rubber Company's New York show rooms — and spent the next nine years seeking a way to stabilise rubber. Eventually he found that by mixing the solution with sulphur and exposing it to very high temperatures it became less sensitive to ordinary change. He patented his idea on 30 June, 1844 — but wily old T. Hancock had beaten him to it by a fortnight! Hancock patented the identical method in England, since when it has been a subject of debate, on

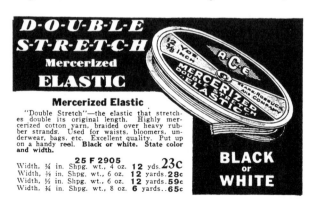

both sides of the Atlantic, as to who was the true winner. Goodyear, silly chap, may have unwittingly given T.H. a clue when, in 1842, he sent a sample of his work to England to try to get sponsors.

Anyway, it was Hancock who thought of the term 'vulcanisation' (after Vulcan, the Roman god of the forge) and transformed the use of latex. In 1851 the Great Exhibition, Prince Albert's pride and joy, devoted a large section to the product and the committee commented:

> From the moment in which vulcanisation of India rubber first became known, all the incon-venience which ordinary caoutchouc presented having disappeared, its employment received an extension which is continually increasing and each year sees new application of this product spring into use.

Who says the Victorians didn't have a sense of humour?

At least one new product had sprung as early as 1844: vulcanised rubber garters. Elastic, the magic web, was in business — and it was good business, too.

The public, gripped with enthusiasm, bought yards of elastic over the haberdashery counters. It was splendid stuff, coming in several widths (there were certainly

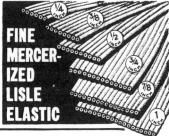

The best quality "Reelastic" mercerized lisle. A woven elastic that gives excellent service. Extra heavy rubber strands, interwoven with mercerized t h r e a d. **Black or white. State color and width.**

25 F 2910			
Width	Shpg. Wt.		
¼ in.	4 yds.	2 oz.	Yd 5c
⅜ in.	4 yds.	2 oz.	Yd. 6c
½ in.	3 yds.	2 oz.	Yd. 6c
¾ in.	2 yds.	2 oz.	Yd. 8c
⅞ in.	2 yds.	2 oz.	Yd.10c
1 in.	2 yds.	2 oz.	Yd.10c

"Lastex" Boilproof Mercerized Elastic

A new elastic that will give longer wear because of a new method of construction. The live rubber strands in "Lastex" are spun round and smooth, over which the mercerized cotton is braided. This enables it to hold its elasticity better than ordinary elastic. Colors: White, black or tea rose. State color and width.

25 F 2923—Width.-¼ in. **12** yards. Shpg. wt., 4 oz...........**35c**
Width, ⅜ in. **12** yards. Shpg. wt., 6 oz................**49c**

more varieties on sale than now), made in cotton, silk, mohair, in black, white or coloured, plain or fancy, stripey or patterned, in strong 'Victorian' colours of yellow, royal blue, scarlet and magenta — by heck, it were champion!

But to keep the stock rolling, elastic still provided customers with a few awkward traits that meant they were always rushing off to buy a few yards more, 'just in case'. It needed 'plenty of air' when stored for if kept too long in tins or other airtight containers it dried out and became crumbly. Nor did it like washing overmuch and positively rebelled at being put in the copper and 'boiled' — think of all those knickers with elastic that 'went'. So it was 'worn at the owner's risk' until the Dunlop Rubber Company of America finally sorted out all elastic's deterioration problems and by 1925 had achieved the impossible and made it 'boil-proof'.

The long, hard, drawn-out struggle had not been in vain.

TWELVE

A STORY OF SUSPENSE

Cecilia slowly sewed six sexy suspenders to
Her silky suspender belt
So that some of her sincerest suitors should
Surrender to sin.

Although women bought the wonderful woven elastic and made their own garters, they could be obtained ready-made. Of one-inch wide bright pink or red elastic, with engraved gilt buckles and taffeta ends, these handsome articles were popular and, it was stated, 'beneficial to health' since all other garters were now condemned as being worn so tight that they impeded the circulation and caused varicose veins. Knitted garters, however, were still acceptable — and some sturdy patterns were published in ladies' journals up to the end of the century.

But a change was in the air . . . In a French magazine of 1862 is an advertisement for garters with 'Parisian

Buckles'. There is just a suggestion that these are more than common or garden garters, more your hot-house variety. Parisian garters had ribbons that attached to or clasped the bottom edge of the corset and, slotting through the buckles, helped to support the stockings. It's decidedly 'belt and braces' but it marked an important milestone.

Elastic stocking suspenders attached to the front tabs of the stays (posh word for corset), are to be found registered for patent by 1882. There were also lots of different types of suspender belt, as an enthusiastic report of 1893 in the trade publication *Progress and Commerce* makes clear: the all-conquering suspender was a cinch when advertising was aimed directly at the modern girl, the 'New Woman' of the 1890s, and Mr Alf Breese, of 34 Brewer Street, London, W1, had a snappy line in suspender selling:

> Mr Breese, though young, has displayed a capacity for business which entitles him to rank among the pioneers of the mercantile world ... take, for instance, the Ladies' Shaped Band Stocking-Suspender; by the aid of these ingenious and comfortable contrivances, garters are entirely dispensed with, and ladies fond of athletic and outdoor exercises have found them a boon which no persuasion would bring them to relinquish.
>
> This daintily got up suspender is made in different forms, and of a variety of suitable materials, and is fitted with the HOVEN CLIP, whose grip is bull-dog in tenacity.

Fashionable women's magazines took up the cry

for suspender belts: 'Garters? Why, these are almost things of the past, suspenders having superseded them; the suspender is made in satin and elastic with gilt mounts and clips, with a shaped belt fitting round the corset.' Suspenders could also be bought in a style that simply buttoned onto the corset. Even so, less fashionable, or poorer, women continued to embrace their knees with an elastic band.

Button Clasp Hose Supporters.

The Button Fastener is very simple. It does not tear the stocking; cannot slip. Our Supporters are made of best quality elastic. Colors black and white.

25312 Ladies' Single Strap Stocking Supporters. Per pair, 5c; per dozen ... 50c

25314 Child's Double Strap Stocking Supporters. Per pair, 6c; per dozen ... 60c

25316 Misses' Double Strap Supporters. Per pair, 8c; per dozen 80c

25318 Young Ladies' Double Strap Stocking Supporters. Per pair 9c. Per dozen...... $0.95

25320 Ladies' Double Strap Hose Supporters. Pair 10c. Dozen $1.00

NOTE.— Ordinary elastic when used for garters or hose supporters, binds and is injurious, stops the circulation. People having used our button fastener hose supporters are never without them. Send for some with your next order.

25322 Ladies' Belts with hose supporters. Per pair ... 18c. Per dozen...... $1.90

During the 1880s stockings were generally cotton or wool (ribbed cashmere if wealthy) for day and plain coloured with contrasting clocks were usual. The heavy bustled dresses were toe-length for morning, and 'tea time visiting' meant slipping into something more uncomfortable and elaborate — including the hose. These were quite stunning! Dyed silk, often matching the rest of the outfit, in every shade with fanciful designs and deep embroideries up the front of the leg.

Red silk, with flights of swallows, pale and interesting yellow wreathed in butterflies or garlands of flowers — these noted to be 'the acme of sweetness' — while for daring girls, known to be 'fast', there were embroidered snakes that coiled sexily around the calves. However, 'nice girls' in society took guidance from their betters and stuck to the golden rule that 'however shapely the limbs or elegant the stockings they are both better concealed'.

By about 1888 black stockings had become fashionable for both day and night. This may have been partly for practical reasons: working girls in towns and cities, travelling on public transport, generally have less time to care for pale stockings — and, of course, black dying techniques had improved. All classes of women now enjoyed more leisure pursuits and 'special' stockings were worn for walking, bicycling, motoring and sport. Black stockings went not only with tennis dress — but also bathing costumes!

Dense black silk stocking c1870–90 with embroidered orange spots. The owner's name, E. Hanbury, sewn on a label inside the welt. Date and set number were often included, so they could be worn in rotation.

By the 1890s the vast range of hosiery on offer was overwhelming. If you had the money the choice and quality were spectacular. The Naughty Nineties (or the Gay Nineties as they were innocently referred to at the time) were the years when upper and middle class clothes were unsurpassed in beauty, the technical details superb — the garment industry catered for the 'haves' with some care.

This decade provided the 'jump-off' point for modern womanhood. Women of all classes came to understand their need and right to be educated and new freedoms began to filter into their everyday lives — reflected in the clothes they wore. Cheaper off-the-peg styles could be bought and fashion news was reaching working-class girls via magazines and periodicals. The beauties in the theatre and High Society were much copied.

This was the Decade of the Petticoat! Sensational, be-witching, flounce-rustling underskirts that signified, with 'frou-frou' of silk against silk, the presence of a lady ... but one with passionate depths! No wonder it was also the hey-day of the hammock. 'Hammocking' could be very effective for girls with tiny waists and willowy hips lead-ing down to a fetching pair of ankles in a froth of petticoat. As with the swing a century previous, this seductive pic-ture was a becoming sexual turn-on for the lucky lads of the Nineties.

But there was a subliminal disturbance to these ladylike layers as the fashion for sus-penders caught on and the

level of male expectation — not to mention their temperature — rose. Attention was now focused on decidedly impure territory — the thighs.

Suspenders, once invented, took a definitive place, not only in fashion, but in the history of eroticism. They have become part of that culture mainly due to the can-can dancers of Paris in the mid-1890s, and we all know what they looked like, don't we? Vivacious, high-kicking, dancing girls in full skirts and frilly petticoats which they lifted to display not only knickers to match — but, lawks, a flash of bare thighs traversed by black suspenders catching up their black (of course) stockings. An indelible image — forever!

I hardly like to mention this, but it is quite possible that the early can-can (the word means 'gossip') dancers actually wore gartered stockings — but this detail has been blurred in favour of the sexy suspenders.

Who would have thought that when suspenders danced and kicked their way into history at the Moulin Rouge they would have developed such a hold on the imagination? Certainly, from that date and into the early years of the 1900s, suspenders in every type, shape or form come into their own. Every sort of

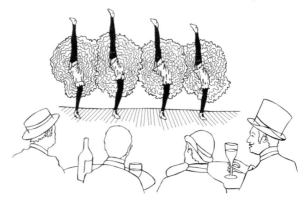

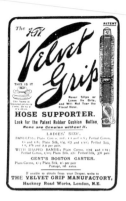

cunning arrangement is advertised, from the sublime to the ridiculously complicated. Such marvels as the 'Portia' Combined Stocking Suspender and Shoulder Harness, which in 1900 is described as 'very useful for little boys'. There is the 'Hookon' Hose Supporter, manufactured by Kleinerts (the 'underarm' dress shield company), and the HW Velvet Grip Hose Supporter with 'patent rubber cushion button' — both from 1906. The garter was still hanging-on-in: *Home Chat* in 1895 advertises the Duchess Stocking Retainer (only duchesses have retainers) which claimed to 'entirely supersede every kind of elastic buckle, clip or band, as The 20th century garter'. This appears to have been made of feather-weight aluminium that 'will never tarnish or wear out'.

There was an every-growing market for fashionable stockings, advertised not only in magazines, but in newspapers, theatre programmes and shop catalogues. Black remained the 'in' colour, frequently still embroidered up the front in bright silks. Stockings were still fairly short in the leg, and therefore suspenders, which by the late 1890s were attached to the front two tabs of the corset, were exceedingly long, often 12 to 15 inches. These were usually gathered, satin-covered elastic, terminating in hefty, workman-like clips. This meant a bit of inconvenience for women — the effect of the huge metal clips rubbing against their legs was decidedly unpleasant. To remedy this, in the early years of liberation seamstresses were asked to make up drawers with bespoke 'holes' worked into the front, so that the suspenders threaded through and out over the top of a protecting flange of knicker-leg before reaching down to clip hold of the stocking welt.

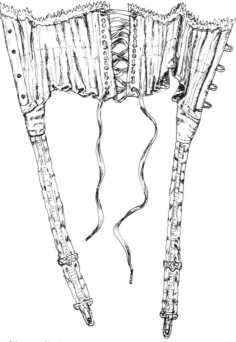

Fine white twilled cotton 'waspie' suspender belt, c1895, with 28 'cased' whalebones and back lacing. The two suspenders are 14 inches long, and set with Art Nouveau buckles, clips and 'sliding' studs.

It is said that the demise of the wooden lavatory seat was hastened by suspenders — the metal clips caused severe splintering of the polished surface.

Mind you, one way to keep stockings hoisted, known to schoolgirls throughout the world in the first half of the twentieth century, was a coin or button, placed against the welt, given a twist and then tucked firmly inside, clamped to the leg. Apart from permanently indented thighs, this seemed to work...

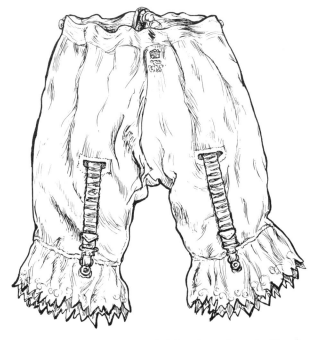

A pair of fine lawn upper-crust knickers (note the embroidered coronet over the initials) with side-button fastening and back drawstring. Superbly hand sewn with two neatly worked 'holes' to allow the suspenders access to the stocking-tops. c1900.

THIRTEEN
ENCOUNTERING THE GOODS

The very dowdy and common-place style of dress should be avoided; there should always be visible, through every change, the lady.

The Habits of Good Society, c 1858

Thousands of drapers, haberdashers, general and fancy goods shops sold hosiery all over the country at the turn of the century, but every big town also boasted a prestigious department store which included areas devoted to stockings and ladies' underwear. London harboured an impressive fleet by 1901, the year of Victoria's death — established names such as Dickins & Jones, Swan & Edgar, Debenham & Freebody, Marshall & Snelgrove, Jay's, Peter Robinson's, Bourne & Hollingsworth, Selfridges, Liberty & Co, Harvey Nichols and, of course, Harrod's, which had started as a small grocery shop in the Brompton Road in 1849.

It is fascinating to ponder the psychological reason why ladies' underwear — including all corsetry — was confined to the back portion of an upper floor, discreetly camouflaged against the unexpected appearance of a man, while stockings, on dummy legs, were boldly displayed on the ground floor within eye-assaulting distance of the main entrance. This arrangement exists in major stores to this day, and close by will be found the haberdashery shelves, neat trays of buttons, buckles, braids, ribbons, thread, embroidery silks, elastic and — in earlier decades — garters. All these much-needed domestic items were to be found not a stone's throw from the stocking counter . . . and that proximity is the key.

Historically, when hosiery was part and parcel of the haberdashery trades, all the goods were mixed together — sewing stuff and fancy trifles alongside scarves, lace, gloves and stockings. It was only as stockings began to exert a fashion influence of their own and become a strong seller that hosiery was disconnected from the mish-mash of 'Haby'.

Many stores published mail-order catalogues, including the famous Army & Navy Co-operative Society, showing the range of hosiery and corsetry that could be 'ordered with confidence'. Positive editorial comment was as important then to retail trade as now — magazines were the vital link to turn 'awareness' into a cash sale. It was well worth it: the middle and upper classes bought by 'the dozen', and one woman was reported to have ordered 42 dozen pairs of silk (I bet her husband complained).

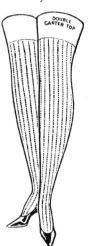

H9715.—Coloured Lisle Mercerised **Hose**, Vertical Open Stitch 10¾d. pair, all colours.

Shopping for corsets — with or without suspenders — was a matter of risking the catalogue selection,

Order by Post with
Confidence. This list
will help you.

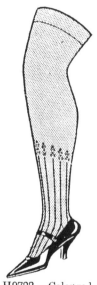

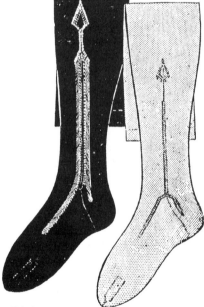

H9722.—Coloured
Cashmere Hose,
Vertical Silk
Stripes, 1/11¾
pair; Colours:
Amethyst, Green,
Grey, Saxe, Mole,
Purple.
To Sketch.

H9723 —Ladies'
Black Lisle Hose,
Lace Clox, 10¾d.
pair, exact to
sketch.

H9724.—**Ladies'
Coloured Cotton
Hose**, embroidered
self Clox, 6¾d. pair.
Colours: Grey,
ole, Saxe, Green
Mand Amethyst.

going to see what was on offer at a big store or being 'recommended' by a close female relative or friend to visit one of the numerous 'Madame' salons that specialised in making corsets for private customers. Older, upper-class women continued to patronise such establishments since it was the custom of their youth, and stay-making was considered an intimate affair between the lady and her corsetière.

All corsetry, whether mass produced or bespoke, was well advertised. No coy blushes here. Some of the most vivid and forceful marketing was that done by corset-makers and their retailers. At a time when a pair of knickers still had to be disguised by modest folding for illustration in 'family' magazines, corsets could zoom into focus with all the panache of an opera star!

The business of cutting and stitching corsets was skilled, hard work, and late Victorian and Edwardian fashions saw the corsetières at the zenith of their technical abilities. Thousands of women were employed in the hand-finishing of these intricately engineered garments; it took strong, neat fingers to handle the tough inner layers backing the luxurious outer material, to slither whalebones and steels into the tiny 'casings', to clamp the metal eyelets into place ready for the tightening laces, and to set the rigid central busk correctly.

Elastic suspenders, covered in ruffled silk, were made as part of the whole stay — or separately as a belt. Detachable suspenders, for use when needed, were available but always priced as 'extras'.

The combined suspender and garter (garter belt) was an American patent in about 1912 and was advertised as needing 'NO CLASP TO GRIP AND HOSE TO RIP'.

By the end of Edward VII's reign (1910) the fashionable shape for women was top-heavy, a large bosom presiding over a long, slender torso and hips. The corset lengthened to support all this, and more suspenders were added as stockings gained a deeper welt and needed an evenly distributed hold beneath the slim, hobble-skirted gowns. Middle- and upper-class girls between the ages of 9 and 15 were likely to sport a set of substantial suspenders fringing their armour-like corsets . . . just like their mums!

FOURTEEN

ALL THE RAGE

The very pink of perfection.
She Stoops to Conquer. Oliver Goldsmith

In 1912 were produced the first stockings made from artificial yarn, manufactured by the American Viscose Company. 'Art' silk, a cellulose by-product of pulped wood — 'originally something to do with trees', as a homely editor explained in 1915 — was to be the first of the modern mass-market materials. At last working-class girls could have some glamorous undies and lookalike silk stockings.

More and more women wanted art-silk hose — and saucy slits were appearing in their skirts to help show them off . . . especially when doing the Tango, Turkey Trot and other slow, slidey dances.

Superb heavy gauge cream silk stockings with lace insertions over the instep and front leg. These charming, festive stockings date from about 1912 and have self-coloured embroidery outlining the lace. This finishing technique was called 'chevening' and first appeared in the 1780s.

In 1917, with skirts on the rise, a writer commented, 'The silk stocking craze has become general because practically every women is earning.' Women earning money! That fact alone is partly why the First World War, however dreadful in terms of human suffering and tragic loss of life, can be regarded as the four decisive years of change for all classes of women. It provided the watershed that many women had sought — and fought for — for so long. Almost by chance the new freedom became theirs, and would be gradually reflected in the clothes they chose to wear.

Like all wars, this one yielded its own crop of romantic exaggerations. By day top clothes were utilitarian, drab-coloured and seemingly devoid of sex-appeal. Many women wore trousers for the first time as they set to work doing the jobs the men had left behind, but there was a good deal of baby-ribbon and inserted lace pulsing beneath the surface, and not for nothing were evening clothes called glad-rags. When the boys came home the girls painted the town red.

'What could be more delightfully sentimental than HIS NAME embroidered on one's garter?' suggested *Woman's Weekly*. Garters, it seems, are always more romantic than suspenders when it comes to the crunch!

In 1924 a competition was run to find a trade name for artificial silk and 'Rayon' was the winning entry. After a timid start with beige stockings, girls' legs came out of purdah and the modern misses of the 1920s went public in pinky, flesh-coloured rayon hose. From this point on, stockings changed from being a more or less unseen item of underwear to an extremely visible accessory.

The conspicuous feature of the decade was the

exposure of the knee, which implied adolescent charm. Unlike the early nineteenth century, the thigh was not emphasised as this would have destroyed the illusion of gauche innocence.

Rayon stockings, alas, were not always helpful towards this image of the bare-legged juvenile. They had a rather shiny surface and, if seamless (the Americans had invented this hosiery technique in the 1870s), with no shapely 'fashioning', tended to pucker in un-youthful wrinkles, a tell-tale sign to those 'in the know' that these were not real silk; it was the same problem that had so vexed Elizabeth I . . .

Speed of stocking production was comparatively mind-boggling by the 1920s: whereas the old-time stockinger, making the legs and feet as separate items, might have completed, at best, about four or five pairs in a day, an operator in 1925, using modern machinery, could produce up to 150 pairs of stockings in the course of normal working hours.

Arkella
Guaranteed

The post-war girl was busy creating a disturbing new look for herself. She wanted something that suited her bid for full emancipation, as unlike the old style as possible. Until 1925 skirts hovered uncertainly at varying degrees of shortness before taking courage and remaining steady at the knee. An immature figure began to emerge — all arms and legs with no curves in between — and this was to be the fashionable shape for several years to come. Popular heroines in plays and novels were described as 'boyish', and young women seemed intent on disguising certain aspects of their physique. It is said, perhaps rightly, that the underlying cause of this overt defeminisation was that, the Great War having swept aside a million potential husbands, girls needed to function within an asexual form. The other practical concern was a determination not to give up the independence (and money) they had enjoyed, as the men who had returned began

taking back their pre-war jobs. The male interpretation of all this was simple: during their absence
women had got above themselves and become
hard-boiled.

The 'Boy Friend' image of the 1920s — dizzy
flappers and bright young things up to naughty high-
jinks — in reality belonged to only a small percentage
of the population. Elderly ladies remained very con-
servative, almost pre-war, in choice of clothes, while
middle-aged and younger women preferred the
shorter length dresses and jersey-knit suits, which
won hands down on comfort and were the direct
influence of the designer, Coco Chanel — but in no
way were their clothes 'shocking'.

Matrons favoured floral-patterned, pastel-coloured
frocks while for parties and dances straight, low-
waisted fluid tubes, decorated or entirely covered
with beads or sequins, were fashionable. The frilly
suspendered garter was often spied (peeping below
directoire knickers) on silk-covered legs, dancing the
night away. The energetic, jerky dances of the post-
war years — the Charleston and the fascinatingly
named Black Bottom — provided numerous opportunities to expose the latest mode in hosiery — and
how it was kept aloft...

> While Milly cuts a caper on the ritzy ballroom
> floor,
> Her sleekly peachy rayons make the boys all
> ask for more;
> Her garters, petalled like a flower, ignore the
> lads' fond plea,
> Remaining still, unplucked, above our artful
> Millie's knee!

American girls wore their shiny pink evening stockings in a curious roll over their garters, while in England and France openwork stockings with eccentric designs were all the rage and hose was often coloured to match the dress.

Fashion now belonged to the multitude; with more money in their pockets, women bought magazines, and fashion and beauty columns were avidly read. The result was that fashion spread its wings and, backed by manufacture and advertising, the images began to change rapidly.

This expansion was encouraged by the film industry. The cinema offered the quickest route to high street interpretation when women were filled with the simple desire to emulate the glamour of a favourite female star — right down to her legs.

Packaging has always been a key ingredient in successful retailing, and the hosiery companies saw to it that stockings were delightfully presented in paper-lined boxes, the lids beautifully decorated; indeed, a box of stockings became an ideal gift and possibly more welcome than chocolates! Cellophane packets appeared in the 1930s and by the 1950s had become very attractive.

Stockings and suspenders have always made compelling illustrations — especially on girls! The French, naturally, had this off to a fine art and some of the best and most sensual were seen in cabaret and theatre programmes of the '20s and '30s . . .

How a woman should handle her hose, the care that should be taken when putting them on or taking them off, is a theme that constantly preoccupied manufacturers — right up to the 1960s. The message that these were luxury goods, not something to be treated carelessly, was frequently emphasised. Smart silk and leatherette sachets were still used to keep fine stockings safely unsnagged, and in posher homes the little maid-of-all-work ironed the hose to make sure they started the day in perfect condition. Classy stockings were still expensive in 1925: pure silk, in a range of fashionable shades (grey, smoke, flesh, filbert and fawn), 12/9; artificial silk, in the same colours, 5/11; woollen sports hose, suitable for walking, shooting or golf, in checked patterns, 17/6 ... so scrupulous care of good stockings was important. Even the wealthy took advantage of professional repair services, provided by laundries until the flood of cheap stockings in the 1960s. Women who couldn't afford an 'invisible' mend continued to darn their own stockings and silk mercers supplied every shade needed for this delicate operation.

The other area of stocking production successfully launched during the First World War was support hose. I'm sorry to mention it, but varicose veins are a fact of life! So spiral rubber thread support hose was the overnight saviour for women who had suffered this painful condition caused by years of tight gartering, child-bearing and, in the case of the poor, years spent on their feet, working, dawn to dusk — and then some!

In his book *Sons and Lovers* the Nottinghamshire novelist D. H. Lawrence draws on his experience of working in a surgical appliance factory to describe with grim humour the atmosphere in this eccentric place with its 'newly pressed elastic web', the flesh-pink 'legs' and 'lady's silk spiral thigh-hose with no feet'. He even has his hero, Morel, chatting up the haughty Clara as she sits making an elastic stocking — and there can't be many embryonic love scenes that have been set in such bizarre surroundings.

The 'big' names in hosiery manufacture in the 1920s are still known to this day: Brettles, Aristoc, Morley, Bear Brand and Wolsey, and many others. At first they had to balance their advertising rather carefully between 'real' silk and artificial — both of which they made. But by 1929 an advertisement for art-silk is full-page against half that for the 'real' thing. The popular, cheaper rayons were winning and silk hose had to use its snob-appeal.

Undoubtedly The Greatest Value in Artificial Silk Hose

WOLSEY ARTIFICIAL SILK HOSE

WOLSEY LTD., LEICESTER.

As ever, royal patronage was worth its weight in gold. An advertisement in *Woman and Beauty* in August, 1936, proclaims: 'NEWS ... HRH the Duchess of Kent wears stockings called 'Embassy', pure silk at 6/11 per pair — this is the kind of stocking the Duchess wore at her wedding day ... and they come from the famous stocking house, I. & R. Morley.'

The best of legs were being called to the aid of the party! For the first time in history silk hose was being asked to step down.

Corsetry, too, came in for a radical rethink. 'Arkella' was the registered name of designs from R. K. Smith and Co of Glasgow who included some specialist models in their 1920s and 30s range.

During this period the mood in fashion became more revealing and sensuous, with bias-cut suits and dresses that owed much to the romantic, sinuous costumes created by designers in Hollywood. Every effort was made to produce a lean, exaggeratedly slender figure and film stars began to look like shop dummies.

Skirts skimmed over the hips and tummy, flaring slightly at the hemline which was well below the knees. The effect was graceful, subdued, and ladylike by day, but increasingly sexy and risqué for evening. These designs needed sculptured, rubber, wrap-around corsets or two-way stretch roll-ons to provide the base on which to mould the tight, slinky dance dresses. The preferred silhouette for 1930 was 'slim but not undeveloped. We must have curves where Nature intended curves...'

There was a feeling for nudity — and in an English summer it was considered very smart to sport a gold sun-tan (because, as now, a lovely tan usually means the money to take a holiday abroad). There was a cult for slimming and health-inducing diets were widely published (does anything ever really change?). Women 'toned up' at the local League of Health and Beauty classes in quest of the fit, slim figure that even maturer women wished to achieve.

And as skirts became longer, stockings, once more, ceased to be noticed.

'Beige stockings are expected for day wear,' comments a gloomy editorial of 1932, 'and for evening as well.' But throughout the decade after-dark sex-appeal was an important factor, and the gowns clung like ivy to the curves beneath. Reporting from a fashion show in 1934, a fashion journalist wrote: 'Each glided past with her suspenders as apparent under her skin-tight skirt as if she had been wearing them on the outside...'

Ah, but, my dear, this wouldn't have happened if they had been wearing the just-the-job 'Zoma' suspender belt, advertised by Kestos and designed to cope with the problem of visible suspies!

FIFTEEN

NYLONS — A GIRL'S BEST FRIEND

We are three spivs of Trafalgar Square
Flogging nylons tuppence a pair,
All fully fashioned, all off the ration,
Sold in Trafalgar Square.

Skipping song, Hackney

In the spring of 1937 a fashion pundit wrote: 'Legs, though no longer as wildly exciting as in the Naughty Nineties, still have the power to charm'.

Lady, you ain't seen nothin' yet!

The legendary name 'nylon' supposedly came out of a dispute between teams of chemists in New York and London, who were working to develop the sponsored research. A compromise was reached: NY and LON were locked together to form a word which, universally, is part of modern life.

Nylon is the result of a programme of experiments started at the Du Pont Company, Delaware, USA. The first successful nylon yarn was produced in 1938 and tested as hosiery the next year. 'Nylons' were launched in 1940 but were available only in America and Canada. It would be some time before British women had free access to these much-prized products.

The introduction of nylon coincided with the start of the Second World War, so all the yarn was commandeered for the War Effort — parachutes, tents, ropes and service equipment — and was not available for frivolous underpinnings.

Nylon is a plastic. Simply put, ribbons of chopped plastic are melted down and 'thrust out' through spinnerets. The resulting fibre is then drawn out, and it is this process that gives nylon many of its desirable properties. From then on it is treated like any other textile. The first experimental nylon stockings turned out badly; they wrinkled in the drying room. However, this was overcome by adding a steam treatment, and after that the stockings behaved well.

Nylon was classified into denier groups, a denier being a unit of weight by which silk, rayon and nylon yarns are measured. At the start, 15 denier was the lightest and resulted in the sheerest stockings. The war had an immediate effect on the fashion industry: rationing of material, including rubber, meant less production; purchases required coupons (stockings took two and corsets, three) and the introduction of the Utility Scheme saw design pared down to a minimum. With severe restraints on cloth, the skirts shortened to 18 inches from the ground in 1941.

Legs were back on parade.

A pair of nylons made in Canada from Du Pont 15 denier yarn, c1940. Heel and seams outlined in black. Picot edged welt, with label marked 35″ — 'opera length'. A wonderful pair of war-time ephemera that have been safely tucked away — and never worn . . . too precious!

Civilian women wore a kind of domestic battle-dress — practical, hard-wearing two-pieces, with a blouse or jumper under the jacket. Shoes were clumpy and unalluring, and early in the war the order went out, 'silk is banned, rayon and cotton mesh stockings only.' Stockings became so scarce — the factories being taken over for wartime needs — that lots of women didn't bother with them and wore ankle socks, or 'slacks'; others, more glamour-conscious (especially when the men came home on leave), used leg make-up summer and winter: either 'something' from the chemist or home-brewed concoctions of walnut juice or gravy browning. Once the base was on — and dry — straight lines were drawn down the backs of the legs with an eyebrow pencil to stimulate the seams of the much admired fully-fashioned nylon stockings.

A woman who worked at a garment factory during the war recalls, 'There was a lot of, what shall I say? . . . funny goings-on and hanky-panky. There was one girl I remember. This was just as war started and you couldn't get stockings. They used to paint their legs with this, like sun-tan stuff and then put a black line down as if it was a seam. This girl — she was a runabout — she was always missing, and they used to find her down in the stoke-hole with the men putting the seams on the backs of her legs . . .'

Early American nylons occasionally reached these shores as gifts from friends or relatives, or via the briefcases of businessmen visiting the United States or Canada (there was a big black market trade), but after 1942 nylons were part of the largesse associated with the GI servicemen stationed in the British Isles. These gentlemen had the power to satisfy more than one war-time craving . . .

GIVE ME THE GIFT OF A GI BOY

Have you got a fag, boy, have you got a flame?
Have you got some chewing-gum?
Like to know my name?

Have you got a fag, boy, have you got a match?
Have you got some chocolate?
I might lift the latch.

Have you got a fag, boy, have you got a light?
Have you got some nylons?
I'll be yours tonight.

The girls who received a pair of American nylons
were the envy of their friends because these flattering
stockings all boasted sexy black seams — an exclusive
definition on leg-wear that became the focal point for
all fully-fashioned stockings when Christian Dior, the
French fashion designer, launched his revolutionary
'New Look' in 1947.

A voluptuous, feminine silhouette now appeared; a nipped-in waist, full bosom and long, wide skirts saw the romantic revival of Edwardian extravagance. Despite political propaganda condemning the 'Look' as 'traitorous' at a time of dire post-war hardship, women adored it and, after years of austerity, wanted to feel pretty and exciting again. The tempestuous petticoats, bouncing at mid-calf against shapely, nylon-clad legs did a lot more to boost morale than any politician's speech!

Following hard on the heels of the full skirts came long, pencil-slim varieties, chic as a rolled umbrella, which were worn with very high-heeled court shoes and absolutely straight seamed stockings ('Are my seams straight?' girls would ask before venturing forth) ... no wrinkles were allowed by dedicated followers of fashion after the war.

You still needed coupons — three had to be surrendered in 1948 for a pair of sheer (this word a generic since the advent of nylons) silk, fully-fashioned stockings, in a brown shade, at a cost of 23/-, which was a small fortune in 1948. A woman I know who married

KAYSER BONDOR

Ankle fit

FULL FASHIONED STOCKINGS

in that year was delighted to get a pair of 15 denier nylons as a 'big' present from a relative.

And what about the suspenders, Best Beloved?

Corsetry had had a pinched time of it during the war, but now, the renaissance of fashion brought women yearning to re-emerge with hour-glass figures like the ladies in granny's photograph album.

Corsets were back in (big) business.

Some of the most ingenious, brilliant and sexy corsetry ever designed comes from the fruitful years between 1947 and 1964. Foundation garments, as they were called, created the outline on which a smart woman's clothes could blossom; from teens to nineties a woman could be shaped. Bosoms were out front: thrusting, whirlpool-stitched bras placed them prominently in view, especially in the evening when dresses were decolleté in a way that hadn't been seen since the 1890s. The waist, of necessity, was hand-span small, cinched down by a 'waspie' that might well be worn over the satin and elastic girdle, a garment that now, to add flourish to the shape of the skirt, often had 'hip springs' — extra padding or width at the sides — completed by long, strong suspenders which yanked the stockings to attention.

Nice girls wore white knickers over this lot. Not nice girls . . . who knows?

Corsetières still made up bespoke girdles and corselettes in old-fashioned, pink broche satin as well as white, black and pink nylon. Teenage girls or very slim women relied on 'just a suspender belt' (these were usually most plain and workmanlike), but for millions of women, the girdle they felt happiest wearing, a friend through thick and thin, was the 'roll-on'.

This cherished second skin of lastex yarn, in white

High-waisted, elegant black and white 'chevroned' girdle, made from panels of satinised elastic and cotton-backed satin with a deep side fastening of hooks and eyes. Designed and made in c1955–60.

or pink — both colours becoming dingy after a few wearings but needing cautious washing in case they lost their masterly control — was first manufactured in the late 1920s. It was top of the class for ordinary women, doing ordinary jobs . . . and you could tuck your vest inside it.

After the roll-on, the next legendary contender to flatten those inches away was the Playtex eighteen-hour 'Living Girdle', which was launched in 1956 and continued to be a best-seller into the 1970s.

Throughout the war, Bri-nylon (British Nylon Spinners) supplies had been taken up for 'vital services', but Kayser Bondor, the name given to their hosiery company, were the first in this country to manufacture 15 denier nylon stockings. By the 1950s the Kayser Bondor label was producing fine gauge stockings in nylon, pure silk and chiffon lisle. The nylon pairs disappeared so fast that it was then the word 'stockings' was supplanted by 'nylons' which, even today, is considered 'slangy' by some.

Thus the fame of nylons was established world wide and great fortunes were made. Dior was the first to produce 'designer' stockings in the mid-Fifties, when exclusive nylons were so precious, so expensive, that 'ladders' had to be dealt with immediately — or else! A temporary stop-gap was a dab of soap or wax, ruination was a splodge of nail varnish — but it was usually still a job for a professional. Gradually, by the late 1950s, this service disappeared because, as stockings got cheaper, women consistently bought replacement pairs (they were never sold singly) and profits continued to rise. A great marketing strategy!

The ultimate authority on the subject of stockings and girdles at this period was the American, 'Miss Manners' (columnist Judith Martin), in her *Guide to Excruciatingly Good Behaviour*:

Dear Miss Manners,

Have you seen the new seamed stockings? I'm crazy about them, but my mother remembers wearing them — she even remembers drawing lines down her leg with eyebrow pencil during World War II when 'nylons' were impossible to buy — and says it was a bore always to be straightening seams. I read in a fashion magazine that straightening the seams is sexy, but it doesn't say how to do it gracefully. My mother says adjusting lingerie is not sexy, just sloppy looking.

Gentle Reader,

Your mother probably knew what it was to have to straighten a girdle, and may you and future generations be spared from ever finding that out. Rearranging one's stocking is an activity of recent origin for respectable women wishing to make themselves conspicuous, as something was certainly needed to replace the dropped handkerchief. Here is the method for straightening seams of stockings: Look shyly over one shoulder while extending the corresponding leg six inches backwards. Lower the eyelids, while slowly pushing the hand down the leg — remembering to keep the posterior tucked sideways and under — until reaching the heel. Then move the hand slowly back up along the line of the seam, undulating it under the pretext of straightening the seam.

Anyone Looking?

Avoid awkward moments when a suspender slips. You can rely on the firm but gentle grip of

Sphere LADIES SUSPENDERS

Dear Miss Manners,

In talking about stocking seam straightening, you commented, 'Your mother probably knew what it was to have to straighten a girdle, and may you and future generations be spared from finding out.' You really must be some kind of Women's Lib. kook! Too bad your mother didn't tell you that even fashion models wear girdles to give their dress a smoother look! Who wants to see idiots like you let it all hang out! A lot of women without a girdle look like the south end of a hippopotamus going north! Even skinny women from the rear look like a bowl of Jell-O being shook! With women like you advising them, no wonder we see girls pregnant without being married.

Gentle Reader,

Miss Manners may not be skinny, but at least she does not have the impression that girdles prevent pregnancy.

Touché!

SIXTEEN

CHANGE AND DECAY

The play-house Puncks, who in loose undress
Each night receive some Cullie's soft address...
Poor Pensive Punck. John Dryden

By the late 1950s the sun was setting on the elegant image of the mature woman. The well-bred model girls, groomed like costly racehorses, still stared arrogantly into the middle distance from the pages of *Vogue*, *Harper's* and *Queen* magazines in their smart town and country clothes — but their halcyon days were numbered.

Youth was about to take centre stage.

Polyester and acrylic, two close relatives of nylon, were developed in the 1950s, as was terylene — all were easy-care fabrics designed for washing-machine survival. The cleverest cousin of them all is Lycra, introduced by Du Pont in 1958 and the most important of a group of man-made elastics, at first called 'Spandex' fibres or elastomerics, but renamed Elastane by the EEC in 1976. Lycra contains no real rubber but is lighter and more powerful than any rubber thread and initially proved itself a boon to foundation wear and elastic bandages.

A Du Pont advertisement for Lycra in 1962 shows an old-style girdle being dropped into a dustbin with the words, 'This picture will start a revolution'.

And it did.

The new girdles were advertised in a caressing, caring manner: 'Take flight from the tyranny of inches. Gentle criss-cross bands flatten you where you most need it'.

But the real revolution was to do with youth culture, it had been growing since the war — the 'Teds' of the late 1940s and 1950s had really started something. The boys may have had Edwardian-style jackets, blue suede brothel creepers and a duck's backside hair-cut — but it was the girls who injected a more permanently effective look into general trends with their circular skirts, tight sweaters, elastic belts, paper nylon petticoats and, worn inside out because the seams stood out better that way, nylons (with ankle socks worn over the top!). These clothes slipped into the high street shops to be bought (or begged for) by the sort of teenage girls who, at this point, didn't know a rock from a roll.

This was the start of little girls wanting to grow up as quickly as possible and be like their big sisters with home perms, baby-doll nighties and a nylon bra from Marks and Spencer.

The Lolitas had arrived — some handling more weekly pocket money than had ever been seen — and they didn't want to buy sweets...

STAY UP STOCKINGS

ONE SIZE
MICRO
MESH
with
SPECIAL
TOP

FIT AVERAGE
SIZES 8–11

By 1960 Kayser Bondor was running a Teenager Advice Bureau to help schoolgirls 'sort out their underwear problems'. Berlei, the corsetry firm, acquired the British rights to 'Teenform', an American range of undies that concentrated on the between-ager — 10–11 and 12-year-olds' bras, roll-ons and suspender belts — all pretty and perky and hitherto missing from the schoolgirl wardrobe (and how!). As they grew up these girls continued to expect the same attractiveness, plus comfort, from their underwear.

The youthful expectation of the 1960s was to remould the look of all foundation wear from then on.

Stockings of the early 1960s retained the natural brown and fawn colours of the previous 30 years, but as skirts began to shorten, 'package holiday' sunshine colours came on the scene. Seamfree, crimped nylons were advertised: ' "Long Life" nylons can't snag, practically never run, stretch tops ... in deep, suntanned shades...' Bear Brand offered a bumper boxful of seamless stockings: 'Ten of a Kind' Matching Micromesh Nylons in 'Copper Bronze' or other well-burnished shades — you pulled them out like pieces of lavatory paper.

'Seamlessly suave and powder-matt'

CHARNOS

Hosiery manufacture was on a high: plenty of advertising in all areas of the media, including TV, meant that sales were meteoric — and were set to get better.

Sheer pop socks were launched to wear under trousers, thigh-gripping, 10 denier 'hold-ups' revealed more of themselves. And then came the biggest challenger ever to stockings — and suspenders!

Tights.

The theatre and ballet world have known about

tights for well over a hundred years — think of all those thigh-slapping principal boys in pantomime — but in 1960 Wolsey started the craze in the high street by marketing a pair of thick-rib woolly tights, based on children's wear and created entirely for warmth in winter. This idea was slowly developed, particularly in America, until 'pantie-hose' appeared as a pair of sheer nylon stockings moulded on to a heavy denier 'knicker'.

The initial change-over from stockings to tights was very slow (many women thought them unhealthy and 'not nice'), but with the fashionable mini-skirt reaching microscopic proportions by the late Sixties, stockings, entrenched for centuries, unquestioned as a piece of feminine dress, were forced to admit defeat. The mini-skirt, by blatantly revealing all, had done away with another long-held sexual demarcation line — the gap between the stocking-top and the very visible knicker leg.

Over-exposure leads to indifference — or so they say . . .

In 1969, when a famous hosiery manufacturer prominently advertised that 'Annabella isn't wearing panties. She's wearing something much better. Charnos Hold-me-Tights', it was the cue for girls to fall in and follow suit. In that year tights had sales of over 160 million pairs out of 470 million pairs of stockings and tights, and soon tights were to emerge triumphant. By 1971 sales of fully-fashioned stockings had dropped to five per cent of the market.

When they had got used to the idea, most women accepted tights and liked wearing them — although I remember a few teething problems in the so-called one-size tights. There were some hopeless examples around, some so long that you had to roll them up under your arm-pits, others so short that the crotch was slung, uncomfortably, between your knees. But these discomforts were soon dealt with and, regardless of skirt length, women opted for the comfort of tights, and roll-ons and corsets gave way to non-suspendered pantie-girdles and others of that ilk. Tights guaranteed the snuggest fit under the silkiest evening dresses or tightest jeans.

Tiny, fragile-looking models like Twiggy and 'The Shrimp' (Jean Shrimpton) were photographed wearing minute tunics or shifts that swept over non-existent curves down to legs clad in lacy or decorated tights shod in small, square-toed, ankle-strapped shoes (like little girl's party shoes) or knee-length boots.

But what incredible legs they were!

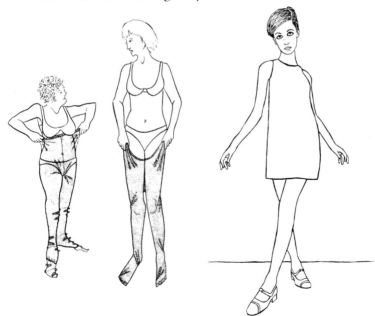

They appeared to start near their collar-bones and go on for miles — long, childish legs, seeming far too frail to support the weight of the miniature body above. Limbs like these were the zest to fashion of the Sixties, and, sadly, not every woman had a pair. This is where tights came into their own: a good pair of semi-opaque, 'witty' tights could cover a multitude of sins.

Realising that legs were to be the erogenous zone of the decade, Mary Quant, that illuminating designer of the Sixties, switched to the right wave-length from the start. She had been commissioning patterned and lacy stockings and tights for her shop Bazaar in the King's Road since 1964, but in 1967 produced her own tights with her famous daisy logo boldly displayed. By 1968 this designer warranted a full page of enthusiastic editorial in the *Sunday Times* on her prophetic brilliance at divining fashion consciousness for dazzling leg-wear.

Ordinary (fawny, brown) tights — and a few pairs of stockings — now became popular rack-pack sellers at outlets as diverse as the local garage, the little grocer's, the paper shop on the corner and Superdrug. Would William Lee have thought it possible?

The 1970s produced more of the same — except that there was a bit of a low for tights in the early years as young and 'young middle-aged' women jumped (well, struggled) into tight blue jeans and then, in complete contrast, got themselves up to look like nineteenth-century American pioneer lasses or Russian gypsies in long, tiered maxi-skirts with layers of petticoats. It was with good reason that researchers for Du Pont in the mid-Seventies asked, 'What has happened to the girdle?'

It was important, as the manufacturers of Lycra, to know the answer.

The evidence they brought back showed that 'rejection' was the key word — in all age groups, but particularly between 15 and 35 years. These women said, quite rightly, that pantie-hose eliminated the girdle because you didn't have to hold up stockings any more. What was more, they claimed that women didn't like girdles and never had, and only wore them because there had been nothing else available. Wearing a girdle had been 'almost a legal requirement' — you had to, everyone did . . . But now, oh wonderful, there was choice. It didn't matter any more. What the heck, they had decided to go 'natural'.

Roll-ons, girdles and all the rest of the restrictive tribe made the muscles lazy. Now women preferred to exercise or diet, or to live in harmony with the body that God had provided. No longer could Paris, your mother or your job dictate what you wore and how you wore it.

Girdles came in for strong feminist flak, too. They

were remnants of male domination (controlling your body to please his eye), they were cheaters . . . a way of pretending you were something you were not. Young women thought that elastic girdles turned men off and were unacceptable as false teeth. However, some women, more realistically, admitted that they weren't all built like a Venus and, for dress-up occasions preferred to have a 'bit of help' around the tummy and hips.

What they all hated and detested were the names: corsets, foundations, girdles, roll-ons — the whole darn lot.

Armed with this information corsetry manufacturers set to work and tried a host of new names: body fashions, body garments, bodysuits, smoothers, shapers, innerwear, outerwear enhancers . . . Co-ordinates came in and 'sets' (which the teenyboppers had worn since the late '50s). In 1976 the established trade journal *Corsetry and Underwear* changed its title to *Body Lines* and Leicester Polytechnic's Department of Foundationwear and Lingerie Design (internationally famous but a bit of a mouthful) got renamed the Contour Fashions Department.

Meanwhile, with bottoms apparently falling out of the market, tights were having a bit of fun once more and sales revved up for the Eighties.

Poor old garters had long since given up the ghost and were almost never seen except on cub scouts, Scotsmen, bank managers or your favourite great-uncle who, having never taken advantage of commercially made grip-top socks, wore hand-knits held up with the suspender-clipped garters of his youth, these looking faintly indecent when chanced on during party-games or at the sea-side. Occasionally, garters were spied on pin-up girls or on brides who opted for old-world charm and wore a lace garter (over tights) just 'for luck'.

The men who hankered for a bit of suspender-stretched-over-naked-thigh treatment were having a pretty lean time … unless they happened to pass a small window in Bond Street where Janet Reger was incredibly busy displaying her latest lingerie designs — gorgeous trifles in satin and lace. This was the stuff that dreams are made of — intimate underwear that held promise of much better things to come, reincarnations of Edwardian splendour … lace-trimmed petticoats, pretty nighties, boned and wired corset basques, extremely French knickers, up-lifting, up-market bras and, above all, suspender belts with, yes, long ruffled and beribboned suspenders that cost an arm and a leg. What genius! What understanding! What enterprise!

What timing.

Miss Reger was a huge influence on the design of lingerie. She had started reviving this flagging market in the late 1960s ('Darling, I looked in the windows of the shops in London and I thought, Good God, how dreadful! I could do better than that!'). It was her suspenders, almost unaided, that pulled this area of British underwear to its feet.

The 1970s always showed a confused fashion picture: the Laura Ashley layers, the ethnic flower power, the blue denim fading fast, the chunky hand-crafted knits bringing back a feeling of the good, homely life in an uncertain world — while at the same moment an underswell of exhibitionism by the inner city gangland and cult groups (of which Punk is the most famous) displayed quite the opposite picture.

Wearing gear that was deliberately menacing and disturbing in appearance, these young people exuded an aura of power over apparently 'normally' dressed people, with an excess of black leather, metal rivets, ripped cloth, tattoos and spiked hairstyles — all the

more outrageous when worn by both genders, deliberately confusing the sexual boundaries.

But surprisingly enough, beneath the metal chains, leather and tatty tartan the girls wore the legendary hose of the chorus girl or stage prostitute — black fishnets (often well-ripped), supported by a barbaric arrangement of leather suspenders dangling from a metal-studded belt — straight out of the thirteenth-century wardrobe of Kings Caspar and Melchior!

The other side of hosiery that continued to grow was dance and keep-fit wear. Lycra, now made in deniers as light as a feather, brought in a whole new kit for both professional and amateur movers and shakers to jump about in. As so often in the history of fashion, something that has been worn by a minority gets moved on into mainstream fashion. This happened with dancing gear: suddenly women who didn't know a *plié* from a *pas de chat* where rushing to buy them because they were the 'in' wear.

As for stockings (now creeping back) and tights, the magic touch of Lycra Elastane dramatically improved not only their fit, but their comfort. Bodysuits were superb, controlling the top for a nice smooth line and giving the 'legs' — including woolly and lacy designs — wrinkle-free cling that survived the washtub. Mums-to-be and new-minted mums were grateful for the gentle pull of Lycra holding up their oh-so-tired legs and tummy muscles in the lightweight 'support' hose that was marketed in the late Seventies — a far cry from the spiral elastic of their grandmothers. In the end not only mums but hard-working career girls wore these sheer delight 'control' tights, for they did great things for the legs, put paid to the VPL (visible pantie line) and kept the *derrière* neat and tidy.

What more could you ask of a bit of plastic?

SEVENTEEN
LAST LEGS

'Always freeze your stockings before you wear them.'
Dianne Brill, super-model

I don't think the hosiery trade could have had a better ambassador for their products than Diana, the Princess of Wales. As she walked down the aisle in her silk Emanuel wedding gown on 29 July 1981, the media had already defined and described every stitch that she was wearing, apart from, on this occasion, her well-hidden hose ... unless I happened to miss their observations. Emanuel, a husband and wife design

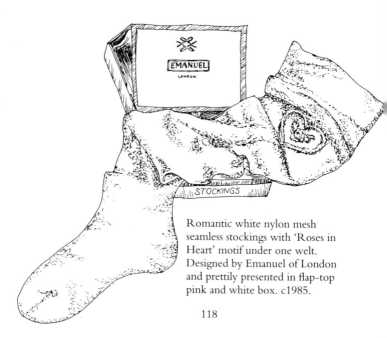

Romantic white nylon mesh seamless stockings with 'Roses in Heart' motif under one welt. Designed by Emanuel of London and prettily presented in flap-top pink and white box. c1985.

partnership, later had the good sense to put their own name to a range of beautiful stockings, but for her marriage the royal bride might well have chosen something different — maybe real silk, which was making a comeback.

As has been noticed (constantly), these particular royal legs are one of the prettiest pair of pins our monarchy has ever laid claim to, and during the first years of her marriage the Princess was seen, ye gods, in green hose . . . and just about every other colour of the rainbow.

There were pink tights for the Chelsea Flower Show in 1984, ivory for Ascot, bright red to visit a police station in 1985, purple to complete an outfit for the opera, pink polka dot ankle socks to watch polo (what would Queen Victoria have said?) and, a fashion that launched a million look-alikes, sheer black seamed stockings with black net butterfly bow complete with red spots, flying at the back of her ankles on a trip to Canberra in 1985.

Spots, patterns, sparkle, ankle interest, colour — this was the sort of hosiery seen around in the Eighties. There were 'hold-ups' that got to grips with you alone, aided by adhesive tape bonded into the welts, sheers with old-fashioned lacy tops and, not surprisingly, a romantic brush with suspenders, these seasoned campaigners having returned to savour — and favour — another generation of thighs.

As top-dressing for women became increasingly hard-edged, recalling the tough years of the Second World War, the skirts started to send out conflicting signals and gradually got shorter and shorter. Hose reacted positively to complete, or compete with, the rest of the ensemble, and thousands of witty, wacky pairs of leg attire were bought from the witty, wacky Sock Shop.

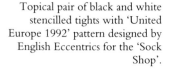

Topical pair of black and white stencilled tights with 'United Europe 1992' pattern designed by English Eccentrics for the 'Sock Shop'.

It was the decade of the 'multiple unit' — they mushroomed overnight. The Sock Shop first opened at an underground railway station in 1983 — and had grown to over a hundred outlets by 1990. They sell a fascinating range of hose, something to suit every taste in legwear — from your ordinary, basic 'everydays' to the wilder reaches of bohemianism (and given that Artwork, Jasper Conran, English Eccentrics and Vivienne Westwood have had designs on their shelves, I'm not overstating the merchandise). Rainbow, tie-dyed, lace, printed, flocked — you name it, you find it at the Sock Shop. At one point, due to too-rapid expansion combined with a mild winter/hot summer and, as reported without a flicker, 'overstocking' (!), the Sock Shop collapsed ... to rise again with renewed vigour in the 1990s.

Although the county 'set' and 'Sloane Rangers' remained faithful to navy-blue stockings (to go with their Gucci shoes), the Eighties peaked with a strong liking for black hose. In every style, the 'ant legs', as my youngest daughter calls them, tramped about like escapees from a Lowry painting. It wasn't just the trad. girls (police, traffic, nursing) who wore them — suddenly, by about 1987 women as diverse as top-notch fashion models and homely WI ladies had got them on, too, from gossamer fine to stomping jersey thick-knits. Black stockings had scored a hit — just as they had a hundred years earlier.

Footless tights and leggings (more defectors from the dance studios), worn with baggy tunics and often replacing jeans, have gained enormous popularity with young women (five to thirty-five), not only by day but, in snazzy, decorative styles, for 'going out' evenings as well.

But beside the mainstream fashion scene, surfacing on the great European catwalks by the mid-Eighties was a more divergent look, with eerie, sado-masochistic vibrations — exposing under as outer wear. Models wearing nothing (much) else but sensational pointed bras, shiny black girdles and French-farce suspendered black stockings — a look more at home in a bordello than an *haute couture* salon (and guaranteed to fell all maiden aunts at 20 paces) — strutted, thighs aflashing, in front of the international buyers and media pack. This visible need to shock — or excite — by means of heavy sexual implications within clothes is usually a sign of festering boredom with dress or society, or both, and this look was further exalted in the world of pop culture with the deviant, confrontational, mad, bad and dangerous to know corset 'costumes' paraded by the American mega-star, Madonna.

So much of that lady's anatomy has been exposed for real, in the flesh or on film, that, bearing in mind 'too much kills it dead', she might have destroyed the whole corset industry single ... er ... breasted. But, no, on the contrary! Corsets — and suspenders — flourished, from tip-top corsetières in Knightsbridge to down-town, naughty knicker shops in Neasden. Ann Summers' cosy house-parties selling erotica in Essex must have been constantly warned of gate-crashers, because 'wannabe's' wanted corsets like crazy.

Naturally, it wasn't long before dear old Marks and Spencer had jumped on the bandwagon and were producing their own outer-wear Lycra hip-slip girdle, complete with suspies, not electrifying by Ms Madonna's standard, but lively for a shop that my mother used to rely on to sell white cotton knickers that 'boiled'.

Everywhere the external girdle was blossoming at

prices from £18 to £200 for a really
posh bottom. Those that 'dared' wear
it in the street said it made them
feel 'safe' as well as 'sexy'.
Perhaps they also carried hat-
pins in their handbags...

I am pleased to tell you that
in 1989, 400 years after
William Lee's initial snub by
his sovereign, Elizabeth II
redressed the balance by
graciously accepting from the
British Hosiers' Association
a pair of white nylon
stockings with scalloped welt
edges bearing the Royal
cipher — so the stitches so
clumsily dropped by one
Queen in the sixteenth
century were nicely picked up
by another in the twentieth.

Fashion now moves out on the
fast track — and legs keep up with
the pace. Hosiery is as constantly
advertised as coffee granules or
cornflakes and the famous names
in stocking manufacture —
some stretching back to the eighteenth century — are still alive
and kicking.

Aristoc, Brettles, Charnos —
who produce wittily named
'Chantilly Seam' stockings
complete with their own

garters — ah, romance still flourishes in the hearts of 1990s marketing men — and Pretty Polly, a manufacturer from the nylon revolution of the 1950s, have managed winning looks for their products via an atmospheric advertising campaign showing sultry 1940s Hollywood movie-stars such as Rita Hayworth and Co, captioned 'The glamour of yesterday, the fit of today'.

Glamour remains a very saleable commodity in the fashion business!

Wolford is another 'modern' company (a family firm, started in 1946) currently producing 30 million pairs of stockings and tights, as well as bodywear, who leapt to dizzy heights of hosiery success with the launch of their Opaque de luxe tights in 1988. These dense, velvety leg-coverings in sombre shades, exactly fitting the mood of the moment, became the cult wear for what's-in-vogue women who used Wolford to underpin the rest of their fashion 'statements'.

Black fishnet, the 'wicked lady' of hosiery, has made a dramatic return, her inky seams 'being the fuse that leads up to the dynamite' according to one wit. Simply every area of hosiery seems covered; design is superb and the techniques stunning. The world of hosiery will, no doubt, always amaze and delight us, but after nearly three thousand years of stockings and stocking-making, you could say that, now, women are spoilt for choice.

As for suspenders . . .

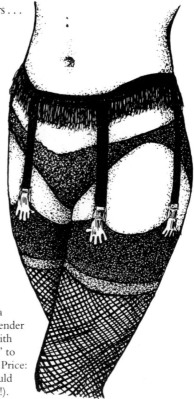

'Fingers & Thumbs' is a black, braid elastic suspender belt, fringe trimmed, with four large gilded 'hands' to clasp the stocking tops. Price: £75.50 (and, some would say, worth every penny!).

Well, thighs kept on aflickering in a recessionary gloom and I get the feeling that while there are red-blooded males at large, these old girls will go on taking the strain.

So if you fancy a fleeting glimpse of 'the other woman', a touch of naughty but nice, then Rose Lewis is the shop for ... both of you! It is a landmark: every taxi driver in London knows this Knightsbridge window! Here beautiful, bespoke lingerie lies close to a fantasy of open-plan bras, tiny G-strings, crotchless knickers and amazing suspenders. Satin, sequins and lace seduce at a glance. It's all very French, very expensive ... but ooh ... so lovely!

There's only one small problem attached to wearing suspenders. As one woman told me, 'They're so darned uncomfortable ... but I sometimes put them on ... just to please him.'

It's a good thing he's not in Scotland. In a recently published report on the lingerie trade, researchers found that 'Scotland had a low response in suspender belts'. It was suggested this might be due to the climate...

Given sunnier climes ... I can't help wondering what Cleopatra might have given for a pair of sexy suspenders to go with her sand-socks ... and her men. Because...

> Suspenders lead to stocking tops —
> And all that's in-between
> Are lots of naughty natural bits
> You shouldn't let be seen...

Ping!

FOOTNOTE

Did you know that old nylons never die? They just
take on new lives. They:

strain jam, soup, paint or port
stuff teddy-bears and raggy dolls
make long sausage-dog draught-stoppers
get threaded through jumpers to hang on the
    washing line
cover hair-rollers at night in bed (charming)
make stocking caps under pantomime dames' wigs
help boost your bra
help boost your fan-belt ... in an emergency
climb dangerously between tall sticks for runner
    beans to rest on
cut in strips they make bands for parcels
cut up rough they make rag rugs
hold bulbs to dry in the potting shed
are used as masks when robbing banks
and my aunt uses them, much holed, as bird-
    feeders.

And I bet you know dozens more INGENIOUS
uses ...

BIBLIOGRAPHY

Handbook of English Mediaeval Costume, C. Willett and Phillis Cunnington, Faber, 1952.

Handbook of English Costume in the Sixteenth Century, C. Willett and Phillis Cunnington, Faber, 1953.

Handbook of English Costume in the Eighteenth Century, C. Willett and Phillis Cunnington, Faber, 1957.

English Women's Clothing in the Present Century, C. Willett and Phillis Cunnington, Faber, 1952.

History of Twentieth Century Fashion, Elizabeth Ewing. Batsford, 1975.

Taste and Fashion, James Laver, Harrap & Co, 1937.

Dress and Morality, Aileen Ribeiro, Batsford, 1986.

Underwear: The Fashion History, Alison Carter. Batsford, 1992.

Socks and Stockings, Jeremy Farrell. Batsford, 1992.

Skin to Skin, Prudence Glynn. George Allen & Unwin, 1982.

Victorians Unbuttoned, Sarah Levitt. George Allen & Unwin, 1986.

Pop Styles, Ted Polhemus and Lynn Procter. Hutchinson, 1984.

Knitting Fashions, Pam Dawson. BBC Publications, 1976.

CATALOGUES, PAMPHLETS, PERIODICALS
AND MAGAZINES

The Lady's Newspaper, 1848; *My Home*, 1929–1932; *Army and Navy Co-Operative Society catalogues*, 1932–34; *Vogue*, 1936–93; *Woman*, 1950–65; *Woman and Beauty*, 1932–48; *The Queen*, 1900–2; *Theatre World*, 1930–6; *Young Ladies Journal*, 1872–4; Sear's, Roebuck & Co. Consumer's Guide, 1897; *Costume*, Nos 6 and 20.